W9-BMO-9DD

D0123322

SOUPS + SIDES

BY CATHERINE WALTHERS

SOUPS + SIDES

PHOTOGRAPHY BY ALISON SHAW

LAKE ISLE PRESS

NEW YORK

Recipes copyright © 2010 by Catherine Walthers

Photography copyright © 2010 Alison Shaw

All rights reserved. No part of this book may be reproduced, stored in a retrieval system, or transmitted, in any form, or by any means, electronic or mechanical, including photocopying and recording, without prior written consent from the publisher.

Published by:
Lake Isle Press, Inc.
2095 Broadway, Suite 301
New York, NY 10023
(212) 273-0796
E-mail: lakeisle@earthlink.net

Distributed to the trade by:
National Book Network, Inc.
4501 Forbes Boulevard, Suite 200
Lanham, MD 20706
1(800) 462-6420
www.nbnbooks.com

Library of Congress Control Number: 2010926541

ISBN-13: 978-1-891105-45-6
ISBN-10: 1-891105-45-0

Book and cover design: Ellen Swandiak

Editors: Stephanie White, Jennifer Sit

This book is available at special sales discounts for bulk purchases as premiums or special editions, including customized covers. For more information, contact the publisher at (212) 273-0796 or by e-mail, lakeisle@earthlink.net

First edition
Printed in the United States of America

10 9 8 7 6 5 4 3 2 1

DEDICATION

This book is dedicated to a true inspiration in my life,
Uncle Joe (Joe B. Blue).

ACKNOWLEDGMENTS

I asked some talented chefs and cooks who love to make great soups for a few recipe contributions. I am thrilled to be able to include their soups in this book. Look for—and be sure to make—recipes from Jan Buhrman of Kitchen Porch Caterers of Martha's Vineyard; Chris Osborn of Better Life Food, a caterering and food company in Newton, Massachusetts; Cathi DiCocco, chef-owner of Café Di Cocoa in Bethel, Maine; Katie Le Lievre of HipShake Caterers in Boston; Geraldine Brooks, a Pulitzer-prize winning author and experienced cook from Martha's Vineyard; Syliva Hurst, co-owner of the Truett-Hurst Winery in Healdsburg, California; Jim Miller, quahogger, writer, and environmentalist from Martha's Vineyard; and Rachel Vaughn, a private chef from Big Sky, Montana and Martha's Vineyard.

I also sampled some sides that I've included as well. These contributions come from Kate Warner, bread baker extraordinaire of Martha's Vineyard; Rosemary Gambino, owner of Rosecuts on Martha's Vineyard and a great cook; Tina Miller, author of *Vineyard Harvest: A Year of Good Food on Martha's Vineyard*; Jim Feiner, owner of Feiner Real Estate on Martha's Vineyard and a cooking enthusiast; and Lisa Zwirn, a Boston-based food writer and author of *Christmas Cookies: 50 Recipes to Treasure for the Holiday Season*.

Even though I test and retest each recipe, I like to see how the recipes fare in a kitchen outside my own before they are set in stone in a book. I send the recipes out to volunteer testers who follow them exactly as written, and send me feedback. I end up having great back-and-forth food discussions with these testers, and use their valuable feedback to further refine a recipe. The testers for *Soups + Sides* include Ela Guidon, Linda London-Thompson, Judy Hickey, Pat Kauffman, Clara Silverstein, Nicki Miller, Karen Honig, Jean MacRae, and Gail Hansen. I'd especially like to thank Bernie Cormie and Hara Dretaki. Hara, a private chef on Martha's Vineyard, worked tirelessly with me to help create and test recipes as well as help recreate the soups for the photo shoots. Berni, who has gone on to make a living in the food business after testing recipes from my previous book, *Raising the Salad Bar*, has now tested almost all the recipes in *Soups + Sides* as well. I value their feedback, friendship, and invaluable contributions.

Some steady taste-testers include Kate Feiffer, Nicki Galland, and Laura Roosevelt, all of Martha's Vineyard, who sampled soups and sides as part of our writers meetings. I'd like to thank them for adding food criticism to the ongoing literary criticism. I also want to thank Renata Santos for her contributions; Rina Diaz for teaching me how to make papusas; Eileen Paccia for her many ideas and suggestions; and my friend Jacquie Clermont of Amberheart Design.

This soup book, like the salad book before, owes its face to photographer Alison Shaw. I am so grateful for her talent—she's always a joy to work with. We have a lot of fun during photo shoots—eating food and occasionally drinking wine while we work.

Martha's Vineyard artist Leslie Freeman generously lent us some of her beautiful ceramic bowls and plates to use in photos. We greatly appreciate this infusion of new materials to work with. Le Roux at Home on Martha's Vineyard kindly let us borrow pots and kitchen equipment to use in the photos. Thank you, also, to Turkish food expert Evan Fielder of Fielder & Fielder Imports on Martha's Vineyard, for his help preparing a side for the shoot.

I am sincerely appreciative of the expert care and ongoing relationship with the publisher of Lake Isle Press, Hiroko Kiiffner, and the work of Lake Isle's Stephanie White and book designer Ellen Swandiak. I am also in great hands with my agent, Clare Pelino, of Pro Literary Consultants in Philadelphia. I appreciate all of Clare's talent and efforts on my behalf.

My husband, David, and son, James, are great sports when it comes to these extended periods of eating whatever I'm testing. In this case, it was a year of soups—some that made the cut, others that didn't.

contents

Everyone loves soup—
The smell of a simmering pot
draws us into the kitchen, and
sitting down to a bowl of
homemade soup is the perfect
antidote to a busy, stressful day.
SOUPS + SIDES continues the
tradition of making homemade
soups, using the best seasonal
ingredients.

The concept behind *Soups + Sides* is to take delicious, wholesome, home-made soups and make them even more appealing by carefully pairing each soup with a side dish meant to complement—even elevate—it. In addition to great salads or breads, these sides include quesadillas, spring rolls, grain and pasta dishes, and small plates. Think fondly of classic tomato soup with a grilled cheese sandwich, and then imagine Thai Carrot Soup with Watercress Spring Rolls; Kale Vegetable and Farro Soup with Fresh Mozzarella and Roasted Red Pepper Panini; Watercress Soup Paired With Roasted Salmon and Greens. These delicious, innovative pairings will satisfy the heartiest of appetites.

Soups + Sides won't send you out to buy a host of expensive, exotic ingredients that you'll use only once, but it does introduce one or two ingredients you might not have cooked with previously, such as lemongrass in the Asian Chicken Noodle Soup. This book champions underused vegetables and ingredi-ents, rutabaga and celery root, for example, that taste great in soups. Try the Celery Root Soup with Roasted Garlic (paired with a Red Cabbage Slaw with Oranges and Walnuts) for something new.

How did I choose the sides that would work best for each soup? Sometimes, a biscuit or a piece of cornbread is enough of an accompaniment for a soup full of meat and lots of vegetables. For soups without chicken or another protein, the sides are a little more substantial; for instance, try the Spring Vegetable Soup with Arugula and Goat Cheese Quesadillas or a Chilled Watermelon Soup with Herb Shrimp Skewers. For soups that focus on chicken or beef, a side with lots of vegetables such

Each bowl of soup embodies all that is good in food, especially when shared with others: simplicity, comfort, joy, togetherness, and nourishment.

as a colorful salad works best.

Some of the sides are whimsical and fun. Chocolate Biscotti are an unexpected treat along-side a Butternut Squash Soup with a Swirl of Dark Chocolate. The playful presentation of the Honey-Dijon Salmon "Bites," eaten off toothpicks, pairs well with the Quick French Lentil Soup.

Many sides, such as the Mini Pita Pizzas, will work with a variety of soups. The mini pizzas are paired here with the Quick Lentil And Vegetable Soup, but would work well with a vegetable soup or another pureed soup. You can't go wrong with homemade Parmesan Bread or Cheddar Biscuits, both eaten warm from the oven, as sides with multiple uses.

People worldwide are questioning the depend-ence on tasteless processed foods and are return-ing to locally grown foods, encouraging cooking that reflects ingredients in season. Luckily, these are the trends and ingredients that make for the best soups. The mixes of fresh seasonal ingredients featured in *Soups + Sides* include dark leafy greens, brightly colored vegetables (said to contain the most nutrients), as well as supercharged beans and grains and protein-dense chicken and meat. The Beef, Farro, and Vegetable Soup is a healthy example.

Usually, when the weather gets cold or snowy or generally miserable, we think of warm, comforting soups. But now that many whole foods are available year round, we can enjoy Butternut Squash Soup with Roasted Gingered Pears in the fall, Chicken and Escarole Soup in the winter, Watercress Soup in the spring, and Chilled Watermelon Soup or Gazpacho in the summer—proving that soups are for all seasons.

INGREDIENTS

The key to creating a complexly flavored soup lies in a few simple ingredients.

SALT: HOW MUCH?

It seems that no matter what I'm cooking, I always put a good amount of focus on salt. In a soup, salt brings out or heightens the flavors of the various ingredients. Sometimes a soup will taste bland even though it has a pile of ingredients, and all that's missing is a little additional salt to make it flavorful.

My easiest bit of advice for a soup-maker is to add enough salt to a soup to bring out all the elements. In other words, if a soup tastes bland, add salt. Add it a bit at a time, tasting as you go. In this way, you can often see (and understand) the simple transformation salt can make. It can make the rosemary more pronounced or bring out the flavor of the root vegetables. Obviously you don't want a soup that's salty, but that point just before the soup tastes overly salty is generally when the flavors are at their best.

On average, I'd say a typical soup (six to eight cups) needs about two teaspoons of kosher salt. I typically add one half to one teaspoon of salt when I add the liquid—water or chicken stock—and when the soup is nearly done, I test, and add some more, tasting after each addition. Sometimes if I'm not sure, I walk away and then come back to try it again.

Certain soups need more salt than others. All the potato-based soups, such as potato-leek and celery root, need a good amount of salt. Soups made with water instead of chicken stock often need a bit more. A few vegetables, especially beets, are higher in sodium, and require less. Soups containing other spices—curry, cumin, or chili powder—get some of their flavor from the spices and some from the salt, so less salt is needed.

WHAT TYPE OF SALT?

What about the type of salt? Any type—sea salt, kosher salt, or regular table salt—will do the trick of flavoring. All of the recipes in this book were made and tested with Diamond kosher salt, a salt with large crystals that's free of additives. Because of the size and shape of the crystals in kosher salt, it has less sodium per teaspoon than regular table salt, sea salt, and even Morton's kosher salt. So, if you use something other than Diamond kosher, start with the lesser amount of salt and increase it from there.

The differences in the sodium content of various salts make it

INGREDIENTS

difficult to specify accurate amounts of salt in a recipe. For this reason, I give a range of amounts. The highest amount is what I think ideally the soup needs to taste good. You can take it from there.

BLACK PEPPER

Freshly ground black pepper has a vibrant taste with a spicy bite. Preground pepper quickly loses its flavorful oils. Therefore, it's worth investing in a good pepper mill if you don't have one, so you always have freshly ground pepper available. Black pepper adds additional flavor to many soups, including chilis, beef soups, and many of the pureed soups, such as Potato Leek, Caramelized Onion-Butternut Squash, and Watercress. Root vegetables and squash have a special affinity for pepper.

LEEKS + ONIONS

As I was compiling the recipes for this book and writing new ones, I saw the extent of my use of leeks. I thought, I'll either have to go through and eliminate some leeks, or apologize for this love affair. I've chosen the latter.

This whole book is practically a testament to the ability of a leek to flavor soup. In addition to onion, adding a leek always adds more flavor.

To understand the subtle flavor that comes from this upright, sturdy allium, all you have to do is try the Potato-Leek soup. With minimal ingredients—potatoes, leeks, an onion, and a bit of butter and parsley—this soup has a subtle, soothing, delicious flavor.

In most cases, I keep the traditional onion that starts a soup on its course. I simply add a leek for

another solid layer of flavor. The combo works great with some of the pureed soups—watercress, carrot, parsnip, asparagus, broccoli, or cauliflower.

You can use the whole leek—the white, light green, and dark green parts. I typically slice off the inch or so of the thickest outer layer that flares out at the top and use the rest—which, when chopped, yields up to two cups of leek.

Leeks are often sandy and need a thorough rinse. After I slice off the flared-out upper section, I slice it in half lengthwise and rinse each half under running water to get any dirt or sand from between the layers. As I do this, I still try to hold the leek intact; it makes it easier to slice. After rinsing, I either shake the leek or use a paper towel to dry it off.

The longer you cook an onion

INGREDIENTS

the sweeter and more flavorful it becomes. I sometimes like to cook onions for ten to fifteen minutes until they start to caramelize and create a flavorful soup base. Leeks, on the other hand, cook more quickly; they even brown if sautéed too long. They just need to wilt and soften, which can take under five minutes. For that reason, I usually start cooking the onion first, then add the sliced leek. If I'm in a hurry, I will add both together for efficiency and speed.

Because of its short cooking time, a leek sometimes has the advantage over the onion. When I have a stock already made and I want to add vegetables without sautéing first, I'll use a leek instead of an onion. Within ten minutes of simmering, the leek flavor will diffuse into the broth while it softens and cooks. Onions take a lot longer to lose their crunch and strong flavor.

PARSLEY + OTHER HERBS

When it comes to soups, parsley is the workhorse of herbs, followed by fresh thyme. Both can flavor many different soups. Parsley adds flavor and also makes a soup look a little better or brighter at the end. Unless a soup has some other green ingredient such as kale or spinach, parsley is the simplest garnish.

Parsley seems to hold its flavor when used early in a recipe and then again at the end. I might add half the parsley to the soup as it cooks and the rest at the end, either to the pot or to garnish individual bowls. Some of the other fresh herbs, such as rosemary, thyme, and oregano, work best added early. Basil, chives, mint, and cilantro work best when added at the end; they don't hold up as well when they cook for long periods.

Many people have a strong preference for flat parsley versus the curly. I often reach for curly because it takes mere seconds in a food processor to reduce a bunch to a neat small bowlful; flat parsley doesn't mince as well in a food processor.

Dried parsley seems to have little or no flavor, and is not worth adding. Others, like dried rosemary, thyme, and oregano, can add a lot of flavor. A general rule of thumb is one tablespoon of a fresh herb is equivalent to about a teaspoon of the dried. If you have a kitchen herb garden, add both fresh oregano and dried to the same soup for even more flavor.

Flavor Boosters

Salt isn't your only last-minute option to enhance a soup. Try adding one of these ingredients to finished soup for a final flavor boost.

TYPE OF SOUP	INGREDIENT
puréed vegetable	a few tablespoons of cream or crème fraîche
bean or lentil soup	a touch of fresh lemon, lime, or orange juice
Italian soups	freshly grated Parmesan or a dollop of pesto on top

INGREDIENTS

All fresh herbs need to be rinsed well. Because they grow so close to the ground, they often retain a bit of sand or dirt. A small herb spinner works best to clean and spin dry quickly. With parsley, you might have to rinse twice to remove all the hidden sand or dirt. To store most left-over fresh herbs, wrap them in dry paper towels and put in a plastic bag, but don't close it tightly; refrigerate.

CHIPOTLE PEPPERS

In my pantry, I always have a bag of dried chipotle peppers and a can of chipotle peppers in adobo sauce. A chipotle pepper is a dried, smoked jalapeño pepper; it is often hotter and spicier than a fresh jalapeño. These can add flavor to bean soups or Mexican-style soups. Like adding a bay leaf or Parmesan rind, I typically add one dried chipotle pepper to a pot while it's simmering. The pepper stays intact, but imparts heat and flavor before it's pulled out whole and tossed.

The can of chipotle peppers has the same smoked jalapeños, but canned in a tomato-based mixture called adobo sauce. You can dice the pepper and add it, or take one or two teaspoons of the sauce and add it right to the soup. Increase the amount of sauce from there, depending on your tastes.

EXTRA-VIRGIN OLIVE OIL

Most of these recipes call for extra-virgin olive oil. Extra-virgin olive oil is pressed directly from olives, processed without chemicals or heat. It's better for you, and imparts some of its flavor to a soup.

PARMESAN RINDS

The rind from a wedge of Parmesan cheese, preferably Parmigiano-Reggiano, adds complexity and depth to a soup made with water instead of stock. Like a bay leaf, the rind flavors the soup and then is removed and discarded when the soup is finished.

As a flavoring agent, rinds work especially well for Italian-style soups—the vegetable soups, minestrones, some tomato soups—especially when you don't have stock on hand.

Remove the rind from a wedge of fresh Parmesan yourself, or buy a container of rinds. Some markets, such as Whole Foods Market, sell four to six Parmesan rinds together in a container in their cheese department. Rinds can be stored in a resealable bag in the freezer and used as needed.

PROPER TOOLS

Using the right tools in the kitchen will simplify soup making and give you the best results.

SOUP POTS

One of the appealing factors about soup is that it can be made in one pot. So what should you look for in a soup pot?

It's helpful to have a pot that is thick enough on the bottom with good heat conductivity to sauté any vegetables, beef, or chicken, without burning, before the liquid is added. Some soup pots have a double thickness on the bottom, and then revert to a thin layer of stainless steel on the sides. These are a start, although you may notice that after sautéing, the food starts sticking in a ring around the base where the double thickness ends, sometimes even burning.

The best soup pot will be thick on the bottom as well as the sides. One of the best brands is All-Clad. These pots have three bonded layers, a stainless steel layer on the inside of the pot, and a stainless steel layer on the outside. Bonded in between are center cores of aluminum and copper, both great heat conductors. These pots diffuse the heat more evenly, and the thickness allows high-heat sautéing without burning. Onions can be sautéed until golden and beef browned without burning with a minimum of oil. And these pots tend to clean as easily as nonstick.

Le Creuset soup and stew pots have a similar inner core: cast iron, another great heat conductor. Le Creuset pots work especially well for stove-to-oven cooking, such as beef or chicken stews. They are heavy for use on a daily basis, however.

I shy away from nonstick pots. I don't like the idea of gases being released at high temperatures, and I don't like the browning action.

My favorite soup pot is an eight-quart All-Clad—it's the one pot that got an intense workout this past year, as I was testing these recipes. It's wide enough at the base to help sauté quickly, and it's large enough to double a recipe, but not so deep that it's difficult to stir.

STOCKPOTS

I also have a sixteen-quart stockpot. This is a great size for making a large batch of stock. Actually, I borrowed (and never returned) my mom's favorite stockpot. I remember her using it to make big batches of Italian meat sauce. It's one of my few enduring heirlooms and it reminds me of her when I use it.

PROPER TOOLS

CHEF'S KNIFE

Like a good soup pot, one good chef's or cook's knife is also an essential tool for soup making. Half the job of cooking a soup is chopping the vegetables, and the faster this job goes, the easier making soup becomes. An eight-inch knife is large enough to make quick work of cutting through a pile of carrots and other vegetables, but not too large to be unwieldy.

Once you have a favorite knife, try to find a cutlery store or kitchen store near you that sharpens knives, and get it sharpened a couple times a year.

VEGETABLE PEELER

A good, fast peeler is essential for the carrots, parsnips, squash, and the myriad of other vegetables that become part of the soup repertoire. I find the Y-shaped peeler works fastest for me, my favorite being the Kuhn Rikon plastic peeler. If your peeler doesn't work well, get one that does.

ZESTERS + GRATERS

I also find zesters and graters extremely useful in making prep work faster. I've seen a couple of functional brands. One of the best is Microplane: the zesters are sturdy, affordable, sharp, and designed to do the job easily.

The fine grater works best for lemon or lime zest. The coarse grater with holes slightly bigger than those of the zester works best for ginger and Parmesan cheese. Ginger grating can often be tedious, but a good ginger grater does the job very efficiently and quickly. I usually buy a long, straight piece of ginger root, cut the knobs off, and peel it before grating.

GARLIC PRESS

A garlic press offers another short cut during soup prep. I like the way a garlic press finely minces the garlic, so it dissolves into the soup while flavoring.

One caveat to using a garlic press is that some of the garlic inevitably stays in the press, so you need to compensate by adding slightly more than a recipe calls for—especially if you love garlic.

I've used a number of brands successfully; I'm totally in love with my current one, the Rösle garlic press. This German company makes top-quality kitchen utensils (and the price reflects this). Their garlic press stands up to rigorous, near-constant use—and cleans easily.

TECHNIQUES

Whether making stock, chopping carrots, or blending soup, these tips will help you every step of the way.

STOCKS + WATER

My two liquid preferences for soups are water and homemade chicken stock. I know you are not going to make all your soups with homemade chicken stock, so in many of these recipes I use water as the base and work to flavor the soup in other ways.

I try to save homemade stock for the soups that need it most, including traditional chicken soup or a chicken escarole or chicken tortilla soup. In these soups, the rich flavor from chicken stock is essential and nourishing.

I don't find the taste of the boxed or canned stocks all that appealing. They add some flavor, but it's not the same as the real, wonderful flavor that comes from a homemade stock. I also find homemade stock more nourishing, and to me, that's the point of making and consuming soup—it's something that's good for us. If I don't have my own stock, I almost always prefer pure water over a boxed stock. Sometimes this means the soup flavor is more subtle. I encourage you to try making your own stock at least once: if you still prefer using a boxed or canned stock, that decision is all yours.

There are other stocks often used in soup books, namely meat and vegetable stocks, but I don't often use them. I find vegetable stocks not worth the trouble of making them—they require a lot of extra work and often provide too little flavor. I figure vegetarians who would like to substitute a good, fresh vegetable stock for chicken stock in a recipe might have their own favorite recipe. Likewise with beef stock: I've found it to be too time-consuming, though when I have made a beef stock, it usually tastes great in a soup. Instead of beef stock for beef soups, I add chicken stock and the beef itself usually imparts the necessary flavor to make the soup taste great.

MAKING LOTS OF CHICKEN STOCK FOR THE FREEZER

There is nothing like the taste of a homemade chicken stock in a soup. Often, with just a flavorful homemade stock, it doesn't take many other ingredients to make a great soup fast. Unfortunately, it's not always feasible to return home at the end of the day and start a chicken stock for a soup.

What might work better is to spend time occasionally making a big batch of chicken stock that can be frozen in smaller portions.

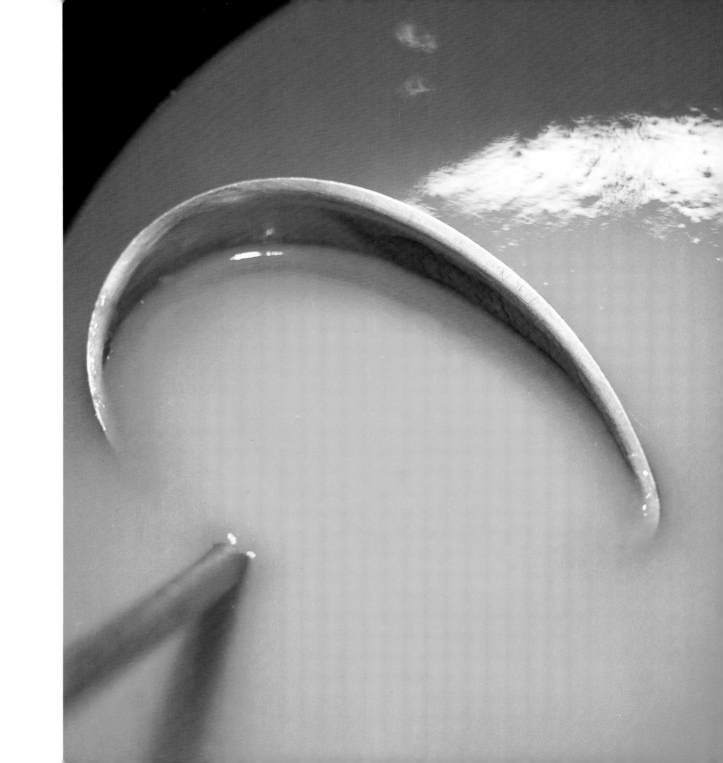

TECHNIQUES

When you want to make a soup, you can defrost the stock and have a delicious, homemade soup quickly. There are a variety of recipes in this book, especially various chicken soups, that can take just thirty or sixty minutes to make with stock on hand. These include the Chicken Escarole with Orzo, Tortilla Chicken Soup, Greek-Style Chicken Soup, Lemongrass Chicken, and Chicken Noodle.

There are several ways to prepare stock in advance. I am going to share the routine that works best for me and leaves me with lots of stock: the Sunday night roast. Since my son loves a roast chicken dinner with gravy and mashed potatoes, I make this at least once a month on the weekends. Instead of roasting one chicken, I roast two and make a soup from the bones. Since I want to make a large batch, I supplement the two chickens and fortify the stock by buying some extra pieces of chicken, usually the cheaper cuts of thighs, drumsticks, or whole legs. Once you roast the chicken, you can make the stock that same day or store the bones in the fridge and make it the next day. A weekend day or evening when you can let the stock cook for several hours seems to work best. (See recipe, page 37.)

I freeze the stock in quart-sized yogurt containers. For a typical soup, I can easily pull out one quart container, or two, as needed.

Of course, you'll have stock on hand for other recipes, such as chicken piccata or chicken pot pie, that call for chicken stock. I always freeze a couple of smaller containers for sauces, and especially for gravy. When I roast the chicken, I use the defatted pan drippings and a small container of previously made chicken stock to make a delicious chicken gravy for the roast chicken and mashed potatoes.

SIMMERING A SOUP

After bringing the liquid to a boil in a soup, the instructions almost always say turn the heat to low and "simmer." What exactly is a simmer? Simmering is not boiling, where many bubbles are breaking the surface rapidly. A simmer is when the liquid has smaller bubbles rising more slowly, every few seconds. In other words, a simmer is when there is some movement in the liquid, some cooking taking place, but not rapid boiling.

While a soup is simmering, it's usually best to cover it partially.

TECHNIQUES

This keeps the liquid from evaporating and leaving you with a thick mass of vegetables. Partially covering means putting the lid on at a slight angle, so a bit of steam escapes, making it easier to regulate the simmering. Soups covered completely often boil more than simmer. If a soup is already thick enough and I don't want any liquid to escape, I will cover it completely and use the lowest heat to avoid boiling.

COOKING PASTA FOR SOUPS

Should you cook the pasta in the soup and hope it doesn't expand in the hot broth, or should you cook it on the side and add it when reheating?

If you plan to consume a minestrone or other soup with pasta or orzo in one sitting, you can go ahead and cook the pasta in the

soup in the last few minutes. If the soup is for later or the next day, or you will have some left over, it's best to cook the pasta on the side and add it when reheating the soup. (I usually cook it on the side so I can control the outcome.) Otherwise, it just expands into oblivion and has an unpleasantly mushy texture.

To cook pasta separately for soup, boil it until it is al dente, (a minute or two before the instructed time) that is, with a slight bite.

After draining the pasta, add a splash of olive oil to prevent the pasta from sticking together. Shake the strainer a few times to distribute the oil and let steam escape—this stops the cooking and keeps the pasta from expanding. Come back a minute later and shake the pasta again, just to make sure all the steam has

escaped. You now have prepared pasta, ready to go into a soup or to be covered and refrigerated for later use.

BLENDING SOUPS

To get a nice creamy consistency for a soup, use a blender rather than a food processor. Food processors blend to a texture that is still a bit grainy, whereas the blender gives a silky, creamy texture. You might need to keep a blender going for a minute or two to achieve the smoothest consistency.

Be careful when blending hot soups: Fill the container only two-thirds full, and place a towel over the top when you start the blender, using the lowest speed at first.

Immersion blenders work nicely, but I often find the conventional blender quicker.

TECHNIQUES

STORING + FREEZING SOUPS

It's best to store a soup as quickly as possible. Let it cool slightly before refrigerating. If you have a large amount of soup to refrigerate, divide the soup into two containers to help it cool quickly.

I like to keep a soup up to three days in the refrigerator. If you are not sure you will finish the soup in that time, it might be best to freeze it.

Many of the soups in this book freeze nicely. It's easy to freeze them in quart-sized containers, which gives you flexibility in how much to defrost.

CUTTING MATCHSTICKS

Carrot and other vegetable matchsticks can look great in soups. Choose a thick carrot, trim the top and tip, and peel it. Cut the carrot on a sharp diagonal into thin oval slices. Stack 2 or 3 slices and cut them into 1/8-inch-wide strips. Use this method for cutting radishes and daikon into matchsticks as well.

TOMATO SEEDING + PEELING

In tomato season, it's great to use fresh tomatoes instead of canned in a soup recipe, although they do still have skins and seeds that can interfere slightly with the soup's texture.

The standard method for removing tomato skins is to slice the tomatoes in a shallow X on the bottom and then drop them in boiling water for a minute. After cooling slightly, you can peel off the skin. I don't often do this. Instead, I usually do a "quick seed." In this method, I cut the top off of a regular-sized tomato or cherry tomato, turn the tomato upside down over the sink, and gently squeeze out the seeds. Sometimes I do this over a strainer and bowl to catch the extra tomato liquid, which I will then add back into the soup. For larger tomatoes, I cut them in half and gently squeeze seeds from each half. After a good number of the seeds are gone, you can dice the tomato. The smaller the dice, the less impact the skin will have in the soup.

CORN OFF THE COB

I love corn, so in this book you will find it sneaking into chilis, vegetable soups, beef and vegetable soups, and of course, chowders. I prefer to use corn kernels right off the cob. Fresh corn kernels have a sweet crunch not typical of frozen corn niblets.

Removing the kernels from the

TECHNIQUES

cob is easy: After stripping off the husks and silk, stand the ear on one end in a large, shallow bowl. Make sure the cob doesn't slip. With a sharp knife, slice down the cob from top to bottom, stripping off the kernels which will neatly fall into the bowl.

ROASTING RED BELL PEPPERS

To roast a red bell pepper, place it directly over a gas burner with the flame turned to high. Char the outside of the pepper, turning as needed with tongs. When the pepper is charred (completely black), place it in a brown paper bag and close it to steam or "sweat" until it is cool enough to handle, about 10 minutes. Peel off the charred exterior, remove the core and seeds, and rinse if necessary to remove any leftover blackened pieces.

If you have an electric stove, place the whole pepper under the broiler and char it the same way, turning with tongs to blacken.

HARD-BOILING EGGS

Place eggs in a medium saucepan and fill with enough cold water to cover the eggs by two inches. Bring to a boil. When the water begins to boil, remove the pan from the heat, cover, and let eggs remain in the pan for ten minutes. Remove the eggs and run them under cold water or place in a bowl of cold water before removing the shells.

OPENING AN AVOCADO

The best avocado for garnishing soup is one that is just ripe, not overripe or soft. It looks better (no blackened spots) and slices more exactly. The outside should be somewhat firm but yield slightly when pressed with your finger.

To open an avocado, cut it in half lengthwise, through to the pit. Separate the halves by twisting them in opposite directions. Remove the pit either by hitting it with the blade of your knife and twisting it out or by scooping it out with a spoon.

After removing the pit, scoop the flesh out from each side in one piece with a large spoon. Then you can slice or dice it. Alternatively, you can dice the avocado flesh while it's still in the skin, and then spoon out the dice.

SECTIONING ORANGES

With a sharp knife, remove the peel and pith (white part) from the orange, first by cutting off the top and bottom, then slicing off the sides along its contours. Trim off any remaining pith, which is bitter. Cut between the fruit segments and membranes to remove each section.

BASIC RECIPES

From chicken stock to soup beans, these basic recipes will add to your soup's success.

BASIC CHICKEN STOCK AND CHICKEN FOR A SOUP

This recipe gives you enough stock and meat for one soup.

MAKES 8 OR 9 CUPS

1 whole chicken

2 onions or 1 onion and 1 leek, roughly chopped

12 cups water

1 Place chicken, onion or leek, and water in a stockpot and bring to a boil. When the liquid boils, skim off any foam or impurities that rise to the top. Turn heat to low and simmer the stock, partially covered. Try to keep the stock water simmering gently but not boiling. After 50 to 60 minutes, remove the chicken to a plate and remove the meat in large pieces. Place chicken bones back into the pot and continue simmering for another 30 to 60 minutes, for a total of 1 1/2 to 2 hours. Refrigerate the meat.

2 When the stock is done, strain out the solids. To remove the fat immediately, you can use a gravy skimmer: Ladle the top layer of soup and fat into the skimmer and let the fat float to the top before pouring off the liquid. If you don't have a gravy skimmer, refrigerate the stock. The fat will congeal on the top and will be easy to remove and discard.

BASIC CHICKEN STOCK FOR THE FREEZER

This method roasts two chickens at once. You can serve some chicken for dinner and use the rest for chicken soup or another dish, reserving the bones to make a large pot of stock. I usually choose the Bell & Evans chickens for great flavor. The amount of water to make the stock can vary; just make sure you adequately cover the chicken. Since it's the chicken flavor I'm after, I don't worry about adding carrots, celery, fresh thyme, or parsley, but if I have them on hand I will add them.

MAKES 6 TO 8 QUARTS

2 whole chickens (2 1/2 to 4 pounds each)

8 to 10 chicken drumsticks or 4 to 6 whole chicken legs

2 onions or 1 onion and 1 leek

26 cups water, or enough water to cover

1 Preheat the oven to 350°. Rinse the 2 whole chickens and pat dry with paper towels. Place them in a roasting pan and roast until the instant thermometer reads 165° when inserted in the thickest part of the thigh, about 1 hour and 20 minutes.

2 Allow to cool. Remove the meat and use for a roast chicken dinner or a soup. (It's fine to leave some meat on the bones; this will help flavor the stock.)

3 Fill a large soup stock pot (up to 16-quart) with the roasted chicken bones and drumsticks or chicken legs, onions, and the water and bring to a boil. Skim off any foam or impurities that rise to the top. When the stock comes to a boil, reduce heat to low and simmer, partially covered, for 2 to 4 hours. A stock simmered for 2 to 2 1/2 hours is perfectly adequate for most soups. Simmering 3 or 4 hours gives a richer result, which may be good for chicken soups that don't have many other flavoring ingredients. Stir occasionally, breaking up the bones.

4 Strain the stock and discard the solids. This amount of stock will cool more quickly if divided into 2 bowls and the pot, or let the pot with stock sit in a sink full of water and ice. *Cook's Illustrated* recommends filling a clean plastic soda bottle almost to the top with water and freezing it. Use the frozen bottle to stir the stock as it cools. Don't worry about skimming off the fat, it will rise to the top when the stock freezes and can be scraped off with a spoon just before using. Once the stock has cooled enough, pour into containers and freeze.

BASIC SOUP BEANS

It isn't always easy to cook beans from scratch to add to soups, and so we often gravitate toward canned beans, which are not as flavorful. If you the enjoy flavor of home-cooked beans, try making a big batch and freezing them in small containers. When you need some chickpeas or black beans, you simply dump the frozen beans right in the hot soup broth to defrost.

MAKES ABOUT 2 1/2 CUPS

1 pound dried beans
1 onion, quartered (optional)
1 stalk celery (optional)

1 Place the beans in a large bowl and cover with 2 or 3 inches of water. Let them sit overnight.

2 The next day, drain the beans and throw out the soaking water. Place beans in a pot, add fresh water and maybe an onion or a piece of celery, and bring to a boil. Turn the heat down and let the beans simmer, partially covered, until soft but not falling apart, about 1 1/2 hours for navy beans (time will vary depending on the type of beans used). Drain, cool, and package into containers to freeze if you're not using the beans right away.

BASIC CROUTONS

Homemade croutons add great flavor and satisfying crunch to soups. You can buy premade ones, but homemade are so much better—and so easy. You can substitute 1 tablespoon melted butter for 1 tablespoon olive oil.

MAKES ABOUT 3 CUPS

1 medium-size Italian, French, or sourdough loaf, crusts removed, cut into cubes (about 3 cups)
2 tablespoons extra-virgin olive oil
1 teaspoon finely minced garlic
Salt and freshly ground black pepper
Chopped fresh herbs, such as parsley or rosemary (optional)

1 Preheat the oven to 350˚. Place the bread cubes in a bowl and toss them with olive oil and garlic; season with salt and pepper. Toss in fresh herbs, if using.

2 Spread the cubes on a baking sheet and toast them in the oven until the bread is slightly crisp and brown but still soft on the inside, 10 to 12 minutes.

BASIC RECIPES

BASIC **ROASTED CHICKEN BREASTS**

If you have frozen stock and need some cooked chicken for the chicken escarole soup or chicken tortilla soup, roasting split chicken breasts is a quick method that produces tender chicken without much effort. Each split breast yields about one cup of cooked chicken.

EACH SPLIT BREAST YIELDS ABOUT ONE CUP OF COOKED CHICKEN

Split chicken breasts (with skin and bones)
Extra-virgin olive oil
Salt

1 Preheat the oven to 350˚. Rub split chicken breasts with olive oil and sprinkle with salt. Place on a baking sheet and roast until just cooked, about 160° on an instant thermometer, 40 to 45 minutes. If the chicken is slightly undercooked, don't worry: it will finish cooking in the soup and will be tender, not overcooked and chewy.

2 When the chicken is cool enough to handle, remove the meat from the bones and shred by hand into thin strips or cut into dice. Refrigerate, covered, until ready to use.

VEGETABLE

SOUPS + SIDES

SOUP SUMMER VEGETABLE SOUP WITH PESTO

Bulging with farmers' market vegetables, this soup is a favorite in the summer. The rind from a wedge of Parmigiano-Reggiano cheese adds complexity and depth to a soup made with water instead of stock.

SERVES 8

2 tablespoons extra-virgin olive oil

1 onion, diced

1 whole large leek or 2 smaller leeks, all but tough green parts, trimmed, cut in half lengthwise, rinsed, and thinly sliced (about 2 cups)

2 cloves garlic, finely minced

4 medium carrots, peeled and diced (about 1 1/2 cups)

1 stalk celery, diced

8 cups water, or more if needed

2 medium Parmigiano-Reggiano cheese rinds*

3 teaspoons kosher salt, or more to taste

5 tomatoes, seeded and finely diced, or 1 (28-ounce) can diced tomatoes, with juices

1 medium zucchini or yellow squash, trimmed and diced (about 2 cups)

1 cup 1/2-inch-long green bean pieces

Kernels from 2 ears fresh corn (about 1 cup)

1 (15-ounce) can chickpeas or kidney beans, drained and rinsed (optional)

4 ounces small-shaped pasta, such as ditalini, cooked (see page 30)

PESTO:

1 cup fresh basil leaves

1/4 cup fresh parsley leaves

1 teaspoon minced garlic

1/2 cup extra-virgin olive oil, plus more if needed

A few pinches of salt

1/4 cup grated Parmigiano-Reggiano cheese

1 Warm the olive oil in a soup pot over medium heat; add the onion and sauté until golden and soft, 8 to 10 minutes, stirring occasionally. Add leeks and sauté until soft, 3 to 4 minutes. Add the garlic and cook until fragrant, about 2 minutes more, stirring constantly. Add carrots, celery, water, Parmesan rinds, and 2 teaspoons salt, and bring to a boil. Simmer, partially covered, for 10 minutes before adding the tomatoes, zucchini, green beans, corn, and beans (if using). Bring to a boil again and then simmer for an additional 15 minutes.

2 To make the pesto, place the basil, parsley, garlic, olive oil, and salt in a food processor. Process until smooth. Add Parmesan and process to incorporate.

3 Adjust seasonings in soup, adding more salt if necessary. Add the cooked pasta. Ladle soup into bowls, add a dollop of about 1 tablespoon pesto to each, and serve immediately.

* If rinds are not available, substitute at least one quart of chicken stock for the water.

PAIR WITH SIDE ON PAGE 44.

SIDE BLTS

Classic BLTs are best served in the summer with fresh garden tomatoes. You'll want to assemble them just before eating.

SERVES 4

8 to 10 slices bacon
8 slices bread or 4 hamburger rolls
Mayonnaise, to taste
Lettuce or arugula, rinsed and dried
2 tomatoes, sliced
Salt and freshly ground black pepper

1 Cook the bacon in a skillet over medium heat until crisp, and lay on paper towels to drain.

2 While bacon is cooking, toast the bread.

3 Spread mayonnaise on each slice of bread. Divide the bacon among 4 slices bread; top with lettuce and tomato slices. Add a pinch of salt and a grind of pepper to the tomato. Top with the remaining 4 slices bread.

PAIR WITH SOUP ON PAGE 43.

SOUP CHICKEN BROTH WITH KALE, PARMESAN, AND POACHED EGGS

This soup is a comforting quick fix for a cold or rainy night. The kale cooks and softens in the chicken broth and the soup is served with a poached egg on top covered with a light layer of melted Parmesan cheese. Serve with a slice of garlic-rubbed bread.

SERVES 2 OR 3

1/2 bunch kale, (about 2 cups, packed)

2 tablespoons extra-virgin olive oil

3 whole shallots, finely minced (1/3 to 1/2 cup)

2 cloves garlic, finely minced

Pinch of red pepper flakes

4 cups chicken stock (preferably homemade)

1 Parmigiano-Reggiano cheese rind, if available (see page 21)

Salt and freshly ground black pepper

2 or 3 eggs

1/4 cup grated Parmigiano-Reggiano cheese

1 Rinse the kale and remove and discard the ribs. Slice the kale into very thin strips (about 1/4 inch).

2 In a medium saucepan or a narrow-based soup pot, heat the oil over medium heat and sauté the shallots until lightly golden, about 4 minutes, stirring often to keep from sticking. Add the garlic, kale, and a small pinch of red pepper flakes and continue sautéing, stirring often, until kale is partially cooked, about 4 minutes more.

3 Add the chicken stock, Parmesan rind, and a few pinches of salt and pepper and bring to a boil. Reduce heat and simmer about 10 minutes. While the soup is simmering, crack an egg into a small bowl. Gently lower the egg into the soup, near the side of the pot. Do the same with the other egg, on the other side. Ladle a bit of broth on top of the eggs, cover, and let simmer about 2 minutes, until eggs are poached but yolks are still runny.

4 Taste the soup and add salt and pepper to taste. Ladle the soup into a bowl, top with the eggs, and garnish generously with Parmigiano-Reggiano.

SIDE GARLIC-RUBBED BREAD

2 to 4 slices rustic bread

1 to 2 tablespoons extra-virgin olive oil

2 large cloves garlic

Preheat the oven to 350°. Brush one side of the bread slices with olive oil and place on a baking sheet. Bake in the oven for 8 to 10 minutes, until lightly crusty. Cut the garlic cloves in half and rub the cut sides over the warm bread. Serve hot.

SOUP THAI CARROT SOUP

A bit of ginger, some hot pepper, a touch of coconut milk, and fresh lime juice liven up this smooth and silky carrot soup. The combo of this soup with watercress-tofu spring rolls is a real treat.

SERVES 6

1 onion, diced

1 whole leek, trimmed, cut in half lengthwise, rinsed, and sliced

1 tablespoon butter or canola oil

2 pounds carrots, peeled and sliced into 1/2-inch rounds

1 1/2 tablespoons finely grated fresh ginger

1/2 teaspoon minced fresh Thai or serrano pepper

6 cups water

1 teaspoon kosher salt

1 cup regular or light coconut milk

2 limes, quartered

1 In a soup pot, sauté the onion and leek in butter or oil over medium heat, stirring frequently until soft, 6 to 8 minutes. Add the carrots and continue sautéing for about 8 minutes more. Add the ginger and hot pepper, and cook another 2 minutes, stirring frequently. Add the water and salt and bring to a boil. Reduce heat, cover completely, and simmer for 20 minutes until carrots are soft.

2 Let the soup cool slightly and then puree in batches in a blender, filling the blender no more than two-thirds full. Add some coconut milk to each batch and let the blender run until the soup is very creamy and smooth, at least 1 minute. Taste for salt, and add more if needed. Return the soup to the pot and heat gently. At the table, pass some cut limes and add a few drops of lime juice to each bowl.

SIDE WILD WATERCRESS SPRING ROLLS

I had never used watercress in fresh spring rolls until I tried fellow Martha's Vineyarder Jim Feiner's recipe that combines the dark spicy greens with tofu sautéed in lots of ginger. Not only do these cold rolls look beautiful, but everyone who tastes them raves about them. Spring rolls take a bit of prep to cut the veggies and make the rolls, but your friends and family will appreciate your efforts.

MAKES 12 SPRING ROLLS

1/2 package (6 ounces) rice vermicelli noodles

1 (1-pound) block extra-firm tofu

1 Bring a pot of water to a boil. Add the noodles and cook for 2 to 3 minutes. Drain, and rinse with cold water.

2 Wrap the tofu in a clean kitchen towel and let sit for 20 to 30 minutes.

3 After the tofu has drained, slice the block lengthwise into 6 even pieces, about 1/2 inch thick. Slice each of those pieces in half lengthwise, for a total of 12 strips.

2 tablespoons sesame or canola oil

2 cloves garlic, finely minced

2 tablespoons grated fresh ginger

Asian fish sauce, to taste (optional)

3 to 4 cups fresh watercress leaves or loose-leaf lettuce, if watercress is unavailable

1 cup grated carrot

1 cup bean sprouts

1 cucumber, peeled, sliced in half lengthwise, seeded, and cut into 1/8-inch thin strips

Fresh mint leaves, slivered

Fresh cilantro leaves, chopped

About 12 round spring roll rice paper skins

Sweet chili sauce (such as Maesri brand) or peanut dipping sauce on page 66

4 Heat 2 teaspoons of the oil in a large nonstick skillet over low heat, and sauté the garlic and ginger for 30 to 60 seconds. Remove to a small bowl and set aside. Wipe out the skillet with a paper towel, add the remaining 4 teaspoons oil, and sauté the tofu over medium-high heat until the pieces begin to brown on one side, about 5 minutes. Flip the pieces over, and sauté another 3 to 4 minutes. Gently mix the ginger and garlic back in with the tofu. Sprinkle the tofu with fish sauce, turn off heat, and set aside until cool.

5 Set up the rest of the fillings in bowls or on a baking sheet on the counter: watercress, rice noodles, grated carrot, bean sprouts, cucumber strips, and herbs.

6 Place a medium sauté pan or skillet (large enough to fit the rice sheets) filled with hot tap water next to the prepared ingredients. Soak one rice sheet in hot water long enough to roll but not so much it will tear, 15 to 20 seconds. As soon as it gets flimsy, carefully pull it out, and lay it flat on a clean kitchen towel.

7 To assemble the rolls, place 1 tofu strip and a small amount of the noodles, vegetables, and herbs on the bottom third of the roll only, leaving about 1 inch of rice sheet uncovered along the sides. Try to avoid adding too many ingredients or pressure will cause the sheet to tear. When the ingredients are in place, roll gently upward one time. Fold in the sides over the filling and continue rolling. Place on a platter and cover with plastic wrap. Repeat until all the rolls and ingredients are used up. You can try to leave the ends open if you keep the rolls snug; it does look attractive with the watercress sticking out. Cover rolls with plastic wrap until ready to serve. These are best made and served the same day. You can cut and decorate them but they hold up better when left whole. Serve with sweet chili or peanut dipping sauce, or your own favorite dipping sauce.

SOUP BUTTERNUT SQUASH SOUP WITH ROASTED PEARS AND A SWIRL OF DARK CHOCOLATE

Drizzling intensely flavored dark chocolate on this pureed fall favorite gives this soup its special appeal. I usually melt a vanilla-flavored Chocolate Mexicano from Taza Chocolate, a local artisanal chocolate maker from Somerville, Massachusetts, with a bit of light cream to give it the right consistency. Serve this with chocolate biscotti.

SERVES 6

2 onions, diced

1 medium butternut squash, peeled and diced (about 5 cups)

2 tablespoons butter

2 cloves garlic, minced

2 tablespoons grated fresh ginger

5 cups water

1 teaspoon kosher salt, plus more to taste

3 just-ripe pears, such as Anjou

1/4 teaspoon ground cinnamon

2 teaspoons extra-virgin olive oil

1/4 teaspoon freshly ground black pepper

2 ounces high-quality dark chocolate

2 to 4 tablespoons light or heavy cream

1 In a heavy-bottomed soup pot, sauté the onions and squash in the butter over medium heat for 10 minutes, stirring often. Stir in the garlic and half the ginger and sauté for an additional minute. Add the water and 1 teaspoon salt, and bring to a boil. Lower the heat to a simmer, and cook, partially covered, until the squash is easily pierced with a fork, about 20 minutes.

2 Meanwhile, preheat the oven to 400° and line a baking sheet with parchment paper. Peel the pears. Then hold each pear upright and cut one side off as close to the core as possible without cutting the core; cut the other side off. Thinly slice each piece, about 1/4 inch thick, and place in a bowl. Mix in the cinnamon, olive oil, and remaining 1 tablespoon ginger and place slices on prepared baking sheet. Bake immediately for 12 to 15 minutes, or until the pear gets slightly golden, maybe a bit browned on the edges. Set aside.

3 Puree the soup in a blender, adding three quarters of the baked pear slices. Save the remaining quarter for a garnish. Season with black pepper and salt to taste.

4 Before serving the soup, break the chocolate into pieces, place in a small microwave-safe bowl, and melt in the microwave, 1 to 2 minutes. Whisk in 2 tablespoons cream, adding additional cream if necessary until the chocolate reaches a pouring consistency. Ladle the soup into bowls, lay 2 or 3 pear slices in the center of each bowl, and spoon the chocolate sauce in a few concentric circles over the pears. Pass the remainder of the chocolate at the table.

PAIR WITH SIDE ON PAGE 50.

SIDE CHOCOLATE WALNUT BISCOTTI

Chocolate biscotti make an unexpected but fun accompaniment to the butternut squash soup. Use the remaining biscotti for afternoon tea, dessert, or a snack.

SERVES 8 TO 10

3 1/2 cups all-purpose flour

1/2 cup unsweetened cocoa powder

4 ounces dark chocolate, finely shaved with a knife

1 teaspoon baking powder

1/2 teaspoon salt

3/4 cup sugar

1 stick (8 tablespoons) unsalted butter, room temperature

3 eggs

1 teaspoon vanilla

3/4 cup chopped walnuts

1 Preheat the oven to 350°. Line a baking sheet with parchment paper. Mix the flour, cocoa powder, shaved dark chocolate, baking powder, and salt together in a small bowl and set aside.

2 In the bowl of a mixer, combine the sugar and butter and blend until fluffy. Add eggs, one at time, blending until just incorporated. Mix in the vanilla. On low speed, mix in the flour-chocolate mixture until just blended. Mix in the walnuts by hand.

3 Turn dough out onto a piece of parchment and divide into 2 pieces. Roll each piece into a log about 8 inches long and 2 inches wide. Transfer to the prepared baking sheet, and flatten slightly. Bake until firm to the touch, about 25 minutes. Cool on the baking sheet for 5 minutes.

4 Transfer one log to a cutting board and cut log diagonally into 1/2-inch-thick slices. Place slices, cut side down, back on the baking sheet. Repeat with the second log. Bake 15 minutes. Turn each biscotti over and bake another 15 minutes. Transfer biscotti to racks and cool.

PAIR WITH SOUP ON PAGE 48.

SOUP **WATERCRESS SOUP**

Like potato-leek soup, watercress soup is subtle tasting and delicious in its mellowness. Adding fresh spinach at the end keeps the soup a bright green. If you happen to have any edible flowers, they make a nice garnish here. In the spring, I use small, edible lawn violets.

SERVES 4 TO 6

2 tablespoons butter

1 onion, diced

2 whole leeks, trimmed, cut in half lengthwise, rinsed, and sliced

6 cups water or chicken stock

2 medium potatoes, peeled and sliced 1/4 inch thick (about 2 cups)

2 tablespoons chopped parsley

2 bay leaves

2 teaspoons kosher salt, or more to taste

5 cups rinsed, trimmed of tough stems, and lightly packed watercress (about 2 large bunches)

2 cups baby spinach leaves

3 tablespoons heavy cream (optional)

1/4 teaspoon freshly ground black pepper

1 Melt the butter in a soup pot over medium heat. Sauté the onion and leeks until soft, about 10 minutes.

2 Add the water or stock, potatoes, parsley, bay leaves, and salt. Bring to a boil, cover, and lower heat. Simmer until potatoes are soft, 20 to 25 minutes. Add watercress, cover, and cook another 5 minutes.

3 Remove the bay leaves. Puree the soup completely in a blender in batches, adding half of the spinach to each batch. Reheat the soup in the pot, and swirl in the cream, if using. Adjust salt by gradually adding more until the soup is as flavorful as possible (this soup needs a good amount of salt), then add pepper.

PAIR WITH SIDE ON PAGE 53.

SIDE ROASTED SALMON AND GREENS WITH DILL AND CHIVE DRESSING

This easy-to-make salad looks gorgeous with the pink salmon against the lush greens and green goddess–like herb dressing. If you don't want to bake salmon, you can substitute cold smoked or roasted salmon in packages—not the thin, sliced smoked salmon, but the salmon that is packaged in fillets.

SERVES 4

DILL AND CHIVE DRESSING:
3/4 cup plain yogurt
2 tablespoons fresh lemon juice
2 tablespoons chopped fresh dill
1 tablespoon chopped fresh chives
2 tablespoons extra-virgin olive oil
Salt and freshly ground black pepper

SALAD:
4 (6-ounce) salmon fillets
Salt and freshly ground black pepper
1 tablespoon extra-virgin olive oil
1 tablespoon chopped fresh dill
1 tablespoon chopped fresh chives
1 head butterhead or Boston lettuce, washed, dried, and torn into bite-size pieces
2 to 3 cups baby arugula
1 cucumber, peeled, halved, and sliced
4 radishes, thinly sliced and cut in half
1/4 red onion, cut into slivers

1 Preheat the oven to 450°. To make the dressing, combine the yogurt, lemon juice, dill, chives, and olive oil in a blender and blend until creamy with specks of green. Add the salt and pepper, and then taste with a piece of lettuce. It should taste vibrant and pleasant; add more olive oil or yogurt if too lemony, or more lemon and a bit more salt if needed.

2 To make the salad, line a baking sheet with parchment or foil. Place the salmon on the sheet; season with salt and pepper, drizzle with oil, and sprinkle with dill and chives.

3 Bake for 8 minutes, then check one piece; salmon should be almost opaque throughout. Bake for 2 minutes more if not quite done. Set aside to rest.

4 Mix the lettuce and arugula together on a platter and top with cucumber, radishes, and red onion.

5 Lift salmon off baking sheet with spatula (leaving the skin behind) and place on top of salad. Pass the dressing on the side.

PAIR WITH SOUP ON PAGE 51.

`SOUP` CELERY ROOT SOUP WITH ROASTED GARLIC

I first made this soup in mid-January when an arctic freeze moved into New England. I'd made practically every other soup in my repertoire. The pure white inner celery root, hidden by it's gnarly outward appearance makes a smooth, creamy, subtle soup. Because I didn't have any homemade chicken stock, I used roasted garlic, leeks, and parsley to help flavor the soup.

SERVES 6 TO 8

1 head of garlic

1 tablespoon extra-virgin olive oil

2 tablespoons butter

1 onion, diced

1 large whole leek, trimmed, cut in half lengthwise, rinsed, and sliced

2 medium celery roots, outside pared off, cubed (about 6 cups)

8 cups water

1 medium potato, peeled and sliced

2 tablespoons chopped parsley

1 bay leaf

1 to 2 teaspoons kosher salt

Freshly ground black pepper

Crème fraîche or heavy cream, to taste

1 Preheat the oven to 375°. Slice off the top of the garlic head, drizzle about 1 teaspoon olive oil over the open cloves, and put the top back on to keep the heat and moisture in. Wrap tightly in aluminum foil and roast until fragrant and the cloves are soft, about 40 minutes.

2 Meanwhile, in a soup pot over medium heat, melt the butter and add the remaining 2 teaspoons olive oil. Add onion and sauté until translucent, about 6 to 8 minutes. Add the leek and continue cooking until it is soft and the onion is beginning to color, about 4 minutes. Stir in celery roots and let cook a few minutes, stirring occasionally. Add water, potato, parsley, bay leaf, and 1 teaspoon salt and bring to a boil. Lower to a simmer, partially cover, and cook until vegetables are done, 35 to 40 minutes. Remove the bay leaf.

3 Blend the soup in a blender in batches until very creamy. While one batch is blending, squeeze out the roasted garlic, adding it to the blender. If the soup is too thick, add a bit of water to get the desired consistency. Adjust salt (this soup usually needs a good amount) and add pepper. Reheat the soup in the pot, swirling in a little crème fraîche or cream to taste.

SIDE RED CABBAGE SLAW WITH ORANGES AND WALNUTS

One of my top salads to eat in the cold weather is a combination of slivered red cabbage and juicy orange segments topped with roasted walnuts and blue cheese. The recipe is adapted from one created by Tina Miller, a Martha's Vineyard friend and the author of one of my favorite cookbooks, *Vineyard Harvest*. It has just the right bit of crunchiness and color to pair with the celery root soup or another puréed soup. For the best presentation, dress the slaw first and then top it with the cheese and nuts.

SERVES 4 TO 6

1/3 cup freshly squeezed orange juice

1/4 cup balsamic vinegar

1 tablespoon minced shallot

1/4 cup extra-virgin olive oil

Salt and freshly ground black pepper

4 cups finely shredded red cabbage

1 to 1 1/2 cups chopped frisée (if available)

3 navel oranges, peeled with a knife and sectioned between the membranes (see page 34)

3/4 cup walnuts, roughly chopped and toasted

1/2 cup crumbled good-quality blue cheese, such as Great Hill Blue, Maytag, or Roquefort

1 Whisk together the orange juice, vinegar, shallot, and olive oil in a small bowl. Season with salt and pepper.

2 Place the cabbage, frisée, and orange sections in a wide, shallow bowl or platter with sides so you can see the colors. Toss well with the dressing. Top with the walnuts and blue cheese.

SOUP PUREE OF BEET SOUP WITH GINGER AND APPLES

This soup makes a wonderful first impression because of its gorgeous color; it's a great first course for a special occasion, such as Valentine's Day. After people comment on the color, they rave about the taste and meld of subtle flavors. For a final touch, swirl a bit of cream into each bowl and garnish with a mint sprig.

SERVES 6 TO 8

2 tablespoons unsalted butter

1 medium onion, diced

1 whole leek, trimmed, cut in half lengthwise, rinsed, and sliced

2 tablespoons finely grated fresh ginger

1 1/2 to 2 pounds beets (about 2 bunches), peeled and diced

6 cups water

1/2 teaspoon salt

3 crisp apples, peeled and quartered

Juice of 2 blood oranges or juice oranges (3/4 to 1 cup)

Heavy cream, for garnish

Mint sprigs, for garnish

1 Place the butter, onion, and leek in a large soup pot and sauté over medium heat until the onion is translucent, 6 to 8 minutes. Add the ginger and beets and stir occasionally until beets begin to soften and ginger is fragrant, about 5 minutes. Add the water and salt and bring to a boil. Reduce heat to a simmer, cover, and cook until beets are almost soft, about 25 minutes.

2 Add the apples and continue cooking until beets are easily pierced with a fork and apples are cooked, 15 to 20 minutes. Turn off the heat and let cool 5 to 10 minutes.

3 Blend the soup in batches, being careful to fill the blender only two-thirds full and holding a towel over the top of the blender when turning it on. Blend thoroughly, at least 1 minute, until the soup is very smooth. Place soup back into the pot to warm, and add the orange juice; add additional water if the soup is too thick. Add additional salt if necessary. Place hot soup into bowls. Drizzle a spoonful of cream into each bowl and lightly swirl with a spoon or a toothpick. Top with a sprig of mint.

PAIR WITH SIDE ON PAGE 58.

SIDE BARLEY SALAD WITH WATERCRESS, APPLE, AND SHEEP'S MILK FETA

This is a nice, simple salad. If you are a quinoa fan, feel free to substitute quinoa for the barley.

SERVES 6 TO 8

1 cup dried barley

1 1/2 teaspoons salt

1/2 cup sunflower seeds

1 crisp apple

2 tablespoons freshly squeezed lemon juice, plus more for apple

1 bunch watercress, large stems removed, roughly chopped (about 2 cups)

3 tablespoons minced red onion

3 tablespoons freshly squeezed lime juice

1/4 cup extra-virgin olive oil

1 cup sheep's milk feta cheese, crumbled

1 Preheat the oven to 350°. Bring a pot of water to a boil and add the barley and 1 teaspoon salt. Reduce heat to medium, and simmer until barley is tender and cooked, about 40 minutes. Drain into a strainer and rinse barley under cold water. Set aside to drain thoroughly.

2 Meanwhile, place the sunflower seeds on a baking sheet and toast in oven until fragrant, 5 to 7 minutes.

3 Chop apple into small dice and drizzle with lemon juice. Combine barley with watercress, apple, and red onion. In a small bowl, whisk together 2 tablespoons lemon juice, the lime juice, olive oil, and 1/2 teaspoon salt.

4 Just before serving the salad, mix the dressing into the salad. Top with the feta cheese and sunflower seeds.

PAIR WITH SOUP ON PAGE 56.

SOUP **SPRING VEGETABLE SOUP**

Some interesting vegetables arrive in the spring that we don't see much of at other times, and this soup takes advantage of them. Fava beans, spring onions, baby carrots, English peas, and morels all give this soup a delicate, fresh flavor. The whole thing is topped off with a mint pesto.

SERVES 5 TO 6

1/2 cup Italian toasted couscous (not regular couscous)*

2 teaspoons salt, plus more to taste

1 tablespoon extra-virgin olive oil

1 cup fava beans, removed from the pods

1 1/2 tablespoons butter

2 to 3 spring onions or 1 large regular onion, finely diced (about 1 cup)

10 to 12 baby spring carrots (about 1/3 pound), peeled and left whole (if small enough)

1 1/2 cups mixed mushrooms, such as fresh shiitakes, morels, or cremini

4 cups chicken stock (preferably homemade)

2 cups water

2 small zucchini (1/2 pound), cut in half lengthwise and sliced

Freshly ground black pepper

1 cup shelled English peas

1 lemon, cut into wedges

MINT PESTO:

1 cup mint leaves

1 large clove garlic, finely minced

1/4 cup grated Parmigiano-Reggiano cheese

1/3 cup extra-virgin olive oil

Salt

1 Bring a medium saucepan full of water to a boil. Add the couscous and 1 teaspoon salt and cook according to the package directions. Drain, shake well to release steam, and drizzle with 1/2 tablespoon olive oil.

2 In another small pot, bring 2 or 3 cups of water to a boil. Add the partially shelled fava beans and cook for 2 to 3 minutes. Drain and run under cold water to stop the cooking. Peel off the second outer layer to reveal the delicate green fava beans inside.

3 In a soup pot over medium heat, place the butter, the remaining 1/2 tablespoon olive oil, and the spring onions and sauté for 5 minutes, stirring occasionally. Add the carrots and mushrooms and continue to cook for another 5 minutes or so, stirring often. Add the stock, water, zucchini, and 1 teaspoon salt and bring to a boil. Reduce the heat to low and cook for about 5 minutes until the onions are soft and zucchini is cooked.

4 Add the peas and fava beans and heat through. Season with additional salt if needed.

5 While the peas are heating make the pesto: Place the mint, garlic, Parmesan, olive oil, and a pinch of salt in a food processor and blend until smooth.

6 Ladle the soup into bowls and add a dollop of the mint pesto. Pass lemon wedges to squeeze over the soup.

* Italian couscous is a large toasted couscous about the size of tapioca pearls made from durum wheat semolina. It is available in some supermarkets or from specialty products importers as well as from some online sources. You can substitute Israeli or Middle Eastern couscous, the large but untoasted kind.

PAIR WITH SIDE ON PAGE 61.

`SIDE` GOAT CHEESE AND ARUGULA QUESADILLAS

You can put these together very quickly to round out this or any number of soups. The recipe calls for the smaller tortillas, but you can also use the larger ones; just add a bit more goat cheese.

SERVES 6

6 taco-size flour tortillas (about 6 inches across)

6 ounces soft goat cheese

2 tablespoons chopped fresh herbs, such as chives, thyme, or basil

1 cup arugula leaves, rinsed

Extra-virgin olive oil

1 Spread 3 tablespoons goat cheese on each tortilla, top with 1 teaspoon herbs; divide the arugula leaves over each. Fold each tortilla over, so they form a half moon.

2 Heat a film of oil (2 teaspoons or so) in a medium skillet over medium heat. Lay in 2 quesadillas, or whatever fits comfortably, and cook until they get a bit golden on each side and the cheese begins to soften. Serve immediately.

PAIR WITH SOUP ON PAGE 59.

SOUP **BROCCOLI SOUP**

The essence of broccoli comes through in this soup, with a touch of melted cheddar cheese added for additional flavor. Fresh spinach keeps the soup a bright green color. It's fun to pair the broccoli soup with the cauliflower soup (see recipe, page 64) in the same bowl—or you can serve each one on its own. See note about pouring the soups together.

SERVES 6

1 head broccoli (about 2 pounds)
1 tablespoon extra-virgin olive oil
1 tablespoon butter
1 onion, diced
1 whole leek, trimmed, cut in half lengthwise, rinsed, and sliced
2 cloves garlic, finely minced
4 cups chicken stock
1 cup water
1 teaspoon kosher salt, plus more to taste
2 cups lightly packed spinach
Freshly ground black pepper
1 1/2 cups shredded sharp cheddar cheese

1 Cut the large bottom stalks off the broccoli, saving about 3 inches of the upper stalk with the florets. Thinly slice the upper stalks and cut the florets into smaller pieces.

2 In a soup pot, heat the oil and butter over medium heat and sauté the onion and leek for about 10 minutes. Add the garlic and cook, stirring constantly, for 1 minute. Add the chicken stock, water, and 1 teaspoon salt. Bring to a boil and add the broccoli. Reduce heat to medium, cover, and simmer until broccoli is just cooked and still bright green, about 3 to 5 minutes.

3 Remove from the heat and let the soup cool for a few minutes. Blend the soup thoroughly (until smooth) in 2 or 3 batches, adding a handful of spinach each time. Adjust seasoning with additional salt and a few grinds of black pepper. Place the soup back on the stove and stir in 1 1/4 cups cheese. Heat gently and serve, garnished with the remaining shredded cheese.

NOTE FROM THE KITCHEN: To serve the soups together, place each soup into a pourable container or ladle. I find the 2-cup glass measuring cups ideal for this purpose. Hold a container in each hand on either side of the soup bowl you are about to fill. Pour at the same time, so the broccoli soup fills one side and the cauliflower soup fills the other side. To create the yin-yang pattern, move each container clockwise slowly.

PAIR WITH SIDE ON PAGE 64.

`SOUP` CAULIFLOWER SOUP WITH GREAT HILL BLUE CHEESE

If blue cheese is not your favorite, substitute some sharp cheddar or a bit of cream instead.

SERVES 6

1 head cauliflower (about 2 pounds)
2 tablespoons butter
1 onion, diced
1 whole leek, trimmed, cut in half lengthwise, rinsed, and sliced
2 cloves garlic, minced
6 cups water or chicken stock
1 red potato, peeled and cut into 1/4-inch slices
1 teaspoon kosher salt, plus more to taste
Freshly ground black pepper
1 1/2 cups blue cheese
Parsley sauce, recipe follows

1 Cut the large bottom off the cauliflower and discard; cut the remaining head into florets.

2 In a soup pot over medium heat, melt the butter and sauté the onion for about 10 minutes. Add the leek and sauté an additional 5 minutes. Add the garlic and cauliflower and sauté 5 minutes.

3 Add the water, potato, and 1 teaspoon salt. Bring to a boil. Lower to a simmer, cover, and cook until cauliflower and potato are soft, 10 to 15 minutes.

4 Puree the soup in a blender in batches. Return it to the pot, add additional salt, black pepper, and the blue cheese. When blue cheese is melted, taste the soup and make any adjustments in salt and pepper. Ladle the soup into bowls and drizzle a spoonful of parsley sauce into each bowl.

`SIDE` PARSLEY SAUCE

You won't need all of this sauce to swirl on the soup, but it takes extra oil to adequately blend the parsley. Leftover sauce can be used on fish, with a few drops of lemon juice added.

MAKES 1/2 CUP

1/2 cup fresh parsley, stems removed
1/2 cup extra-virgin olive oil
Pinch of salt

1 Combine the parsley and oil in a blender and blend until very smooth. Add a pinch of salt.

SOUP MISO SOUP

Miso, a traditional salty and buttery-tasting soy paste used in Japanese cuisine, makes a quick and invigorating soup. Miso varies in intensity and flavor, but the darker, "red" miso makes a flavorful broth just by adding a few tablespoons to water. I love adding shiitake mushrooms, ginger, and watercress, but it's very easy to use miso as a base for nearly any vegetable you have on hand. Miso is unpasteurized and contains enzymes that aid in digestion. These enzymes are best maintained by simmering the soup, not boiling.

SERVES 2 OR 3

- 2 teaspoons dark sesame oil or canola oil
- 12 shiitake mushrooms, stems discarded, thinly sliced
- 3 scallions, white and green parts, thinly sliced
- Salt or soy sauce, to taste
- 6 cups water
- 4 ounces firm tofu, cut into small cubes (about 1 cup) (optional)
- 4 to 5 tablespoons red miso
- 1/4 cup daikon radish or carrot, peeled and cut into matchsticks
- 1/2 small bunch watercress or another favorite green, large stems removed and discarded, chopped
- 1 tablespoon grated fresh ginger, grated on a Microplane (see page 25)

1 Heat the sesame oil in a soup pot over low heat and sauté the mushrooms, scallions, and a pinch of salt or shake of soy sauce, until mushrooms are cooked, 2 to 3 minutes, stirring often.

2 Add the water and tofu and bring to a boil. As the soup is heating, remove about 1/2 cup water to a bowl and dissolve 4 tablespoons miso in it. Remove soup from the heat or keep it on a low heat and add the dissolved miso, the daikon or carrot, and watercress. Squeeze the ginger over the soup to release its juice. You can add a bit of the ginger itself to the soup, or discard. Test for seasoning, and add additional miso (dissolved in more water), salt, or soy sauce, if desired.

PAIR WITH SIDE ON PAGE 66.

SIDE VEGGIE PLATTER WITH PEANUT DIPPING SAUCE

This Asian-inspired peanut dip includes a bit of coconut milk, ginger, and soy. It's perfect with a platter of crispy, colorful veggies, including some Asian veggies like baby bok choy or Napa cabbage that are so sweet and tender they don't need to be cooked, as well as crunchy daikon radish, which looks like a large white carrot.

SERVES 4

2 cups sugar snap peas, strings removed

1/2 English cucumber, peeled and sliced on a diagonal

2 small heads baby bok choy, bases cut off, stalks separated and rinsed

3 large carrots, peeled and cut thinly sliced on a diagonal

3 stalks celery, peeled cut into sticks (optional)

1/4 daikon radish, peeled and thinly sliced on a diagonal, or 4 radishes, thinly sliced

1/2 red or yellow bell pepper, cored and cut on an angle into a thin triangular shape

PEANUT DIPPING SAUCE:

6 tablespoons creamy-style peanut butter

1/2 cup light coconut milk

1 tablespoon soy sauce, or more to taste

1 tablespoon light or dark brown sugar

1 to 2 teaspoons grated fresh ginger, grated on a Microplane (see page 25)

1/2 to 1 teaspoon Sriracha hot sauce

2 teaspoons freshly squeezed lime juice

1 Bring a small pot of water to a boil. Blanch snap peas for 40 seconds and rinse immediately in cold water. Drain.

2 Place snap peas, cucumbers, baby bok choy, carrots, celery, daikon radish, and bell peppers on a platter.

3 To make the sauce, whisk the peanut butter, coconut milk, soy sauce, brown sugar, ginger, Sriracha, and lime juice in a small bowl. Try it with a veggie, and add more ginger, soy, brown sugar, or hot sauce, depending on your preference.

PAIR WITH SOUP ON PAGE 65.

`SOUP` POTATO-LEEK SOUP

Potato-leek is one of the first soups I remember making and remains one of my favorites. I find no need to add cream, though some of my testers have told me they added chicken stock in place of water for a richer flavor. Because I like to use almost the whole leek, along with some parsley, the soup becomes a shade of pale green rather than off-white.

SERVES 4 TO 6

1 small to medium onion, diced

2 large or 3 medium whole leeks, trimmed, cut in half lengthwise, rinsed, and sliced (about 4 cups) (use all but the thick outer layers at the top)

2 tablespoons butter

6 cups water

2 medium potatoes (about 1 pound), peeled and sliced 1/4 inch thick

2 tablespoons minced fresh parsley leaves, plus more for garnish (optional)

2 bay leaves

1 to 2 teaspoons kosher salt

1/4 teaspoon freshly ground black pepper

Croutons, for garnish (optional) (see recipe, page 38)

1 In a soup pot, sauté the onion and leeks in the butter over medium heat until soft, about 10 minutes. Add the water, potatoes, parsley, bay leaves, and 1 teaspoon salt and bring to a boil. Lower heat to medium-low, cover, and simmer until potatoes are soft, about 30 minutes.

2 Remove the bay leaves. Puree the soup in a blender in 2 batches until creamy and smooth. Return the soup to the pot and heat gently. This soup typically needs a fair amount of salt; keep adding salt a bit at a time, tasting as you go, until the leek flavor shines through. Add the pepper. Ladle into soup bowls and garnish with croutons or chopped parsley, if desired.

PAIR WITH SIDE ON PAGE 70.

SIDE BROCCOLI RABE AND CHEESE CROSTINI

You can make these crostini with Mahon, a nice Spanish cheese; Morbier, a raw cow's milk cheese from France; or another cheese of your choice. The dish can be prepared a few hours ahead of time; just keep the broccoli rabe on the side until the last minute. I try to buy the larger baguettes to make sure each slice is a good size, but any type of good bread will do.

SERVES 4 TO 6

1/2 bunch broccoli rabe (about 1/2 pound), chopped into 1-inch pieces

1 tablespoon extra-virgin olive oil

1 large clove garlic, finely minced

Salt

1 wide baguette, sliced about 1/2 inch thick on a diagonal

8 ounces Morbier or Mahon cheese, sliced in pieces about 1/4 inch thick

1 Preheat the oven to 350°. Bring about 4 cups water to a boil in a medium skillet with a lid. Add the broccoli rabe, mix to submerge and boil for 2 minutes, covered. Drain the broccoli rabe and rinse under cold water. Squeeze any excess water from the broccoli rabe and set aside.

2 In the same skillet over medium heat, heat the oil and sauté the garlic for 30 to 60 seconds, stirring. Turn off the heat, add the broccoli rabe, and stir to coat with the oil and garlic. Sprinkle with 1 or 2 pinches of salt. Set aside in a bowl.

3 Place bread on a baking sheet and top with slices of cheese to cover. Bake for 3 minutes or until the cheese starts to melt.

4 Top crostini with the broccoli rabe and place back in the oven for an additional 2 minutes. Serve immediately with the soup.

PAIR WITH SOUP ON PAGE 69.

SOUP **CARAMELIZED ONION–BUTTERNUT SQUASH SOUP WITH MELTED CHEESE TOASTS**

This is a vegetarian version of onion soup, flavored with Parmesan rinds, diced butternut squash, and a light layer of cheese melted on crostini.

SERVES 6

1 tablespoon butter

2 to 3 tablespoons extra-virgin olive oil

4 medium onions, halved and thinly sliced

2 garlic gloves, minced

1 small or medium butternut squash, peeled and cut into 1/2-inch cubes (2 to 2 1/2 cups)

1/3 cup port wine

6 cups water

2 Parmigiano-Reggiano cheese rinds

Salt and freshly ground black pepper

1 baguette

1/3 cup shredded Parmigiano-Reggiano cheese

1 1/2 cups shredded fontina cheese (or Gruyère cheese)

1 Preheat the oven to 350°. In a heavy-bottomed soup pot, over medium-high heat, combine the butter and 1 tablespoon oil and sauté onions, lowering the heat as the onions start to reduce and lose their liquid, eventually becoming golden brown and caramelized (sweet-tasting and no longer crunchy), 20 to 25 minutes. Keep stirring and scraping the pan often to keep the onions from sticking and to incorporate the brown bits that form on the bottom of the pot. You might need a bit more oil as you cook. Stir in the garlic and squash and sauté another 5 to 7 minutes, then deglaze with the port wine (add wine and stir to loosen browned bits).

2 Add the water and Parmesan rinds and bring to a boil. Lower heat, partially cover, and simmer until squash is cooked, about 15 minutes. Remove the rinds and discard; season with salt and pepper.

3 Cut the bread into 1/4-inch slices and place on a baking sheet. Brush one side of each slice with olive oil and bake until lightly crusty, 8 or 9 minutes. Top the bread with a layer of Parmesan and then as much fontina cheese as fits on top. Bake until the cheese is melted.

4 Ladle the soup into bowls and place 1 or 2 cheese toasts on top of each serving.

PAIR WITH SIDE ON PAGE 73.

SIDE ARUGULA SALAD WITH SLICED PEARS AND GOAT CHEESE

In the fall, red Anjou pears or red Bartletts make an attractive addition to a salad. Purchase pears just on the verge of ripeness, but still a little firm so they are easy to slice. The mini cheese balls look fantastic and are super easy to make, but you can skip them if you think it's too much to have cheese on the soup and in the salad.

SERVES 6

SALAD:

1/2 cup pecans or walnuts

4 cups baby arugula

3 cups (1 small head) Bibb or Boston lettuce, washed and dried

4 to 6 ounces goat cheese

1 to 2 just-ripe pears

Freshly squeezed lemon juice, for sprinkling

1 cup pomegranate seeds (optional)

HONEY BALSAMIC VINAIGRETTE:

2 tablespoons balsamic vinegar

1 1/2 teaspoons honey

1 teaspoon finely minced shallot

5 tablespoons extra-virgin olive oil

1/4 teaspoon kosher salt

1 Preheat the oven to 350°. Place the nuts on a baking sheet and toast for 5 minutes.

2 Combine the arugula and lettuce in a wide salad bowl.

3 With your hands and some disposable plastic gloves if handy, roll the goat cheese into small balls, about 1/2 inch in diameter, and place on a piece of waxed or parchment paper on a plate. Set aside.

4 Place nuts in a food processor and pulse to finely chop. Place on a plate and roll the goat cheese balls in the nuts to completely cover, pressing to get a nice coating. Place the cheese balls back on the paper and refrigerate, covered in plastic wrap, until ready to serve the salad.

5 To make the dressing, whisk together the vinegar, honey, shallot, olive oil, and salt in a small bowl. Just before serving, dress the salad with just enough vinaigrette to coat the greens, tossing gently.

6 To cut the pear, hold it upright and cut one side off, as close to the core as possible without cutting the core. Then cut the other side off. Cut the pieces into thin, even slices. To keep slices from browning, sprinkle with a few drop of lemon juice and mix.

7 Top the dressed salad with the pecan balls, sliced pears, and pomegranate seeds, if using.

PAIR WITH SOUP ON PAGE 71.

`SOUP` # BASIL AND ZUCCHINI SOUP

In the summer, this soup offers one way to enjoy an excess of garden zucchini. In winter, it reminds us of the garden-fresh taste of summer. The zucchini, combined with roasted garlic and fresh basil, creates a delicious aroma.

SERVES 6 TO 8

1 head garlic

1 tablespoon plus 1 teaspoon extra-virgin olive oil or butter

2 medium onions, diced

1 large or 2 small whole leeks, trimmed, cut in half lengthwise, rinsed, and sliced

2 carrots, cut into very small dice or chopped in the food processor

3 medium to large zucchini, cut into 1-inch cubes (about 8 cups)

7 cups water

1 1/2 teaspoons kosher salt, or more to taste

1/2 cup fresh basil leaves, washed

Freshly ground black pepper

1 Preheat the oven to 375°. Slice off the top of the garlic head, cutting through all the cloves. Drizzle about 1 teaspoon olive oil over the open cloves; put the top back on to keep the heat and moisture in (and to make it easier to squeeze garlic out at the end). Wrap tightly in foil and put directly in oven until cloves are fragrant and have softened, about 40 minutes. When the head of garlic is cool enough to handle, remove from the foil and squeeze the garlic from the cloves into a small bowl.

2 In a large soup pot over medium heat, sauté the onions, leeks, and carrots in the remaining 1 tablespoon oil until onions and leeks are soft, 8 to 10 minutes. Add zucchini, water, and 1 teaspoon salt and bring to a boil. Turn heat to low, partially cover, and simmer until vegetables are cooked, about 30 minutes.

3 Puree the soup completely in batches, adding the roasted garlic and fresh basil leaves to the blender. Add freshly ground pepper and additional salt to taste.

PAIR WITH SIDE ON PAGE 76.

SIDE OPEN-FACED CHEESE AND TOMATO SANDWICHES

SERVES 4

4 slices fresh French, Italian, or sourdough bread

Mustard, such as Dijon or whole-grain, to taste

Cheddar cheese, sliced

2 fresh tomatoes, sliced

Salt, to taste

1 Preheat the broiler. Place the bread on a baking sheet and spread a light layer of mustard on each slice.

2 Top with cheddar cheese. Place a slice of tomato on top. Sprinkle with salt.

3 Place the baking sheet about 8 inches from the broiler and broil until the cheese is melted. Check often to make sure the bread does not burn. Serve immediately.

PAIR WITH SOUP ON PAGE 74.

`SOUP` **CARROT-GINGER SOUP**

You can make a simple, creamy soup without cream—and this carrot soup is a perfect example.

SERVES 6

1 medium onion, diced

2 tablespoons butter or extra-virgin olive oil

1 whole leek, trimmed, cut in half lengthwise, rinsed, and sliced

2 pounds carrots, peeled and sliced into 1/2-inch rounds

2 tablespoons finely grated fresh ginger

5 cups water

1 to 2 teaspoons kosher salt, or to taste

1/2 cup freshly squeezed orange juice (or more if needed)

2 teaspoons maple syrup

1 In a large soup pot, sauté the onion in the butter or oil over medium heat for 5 minutes until golden. Add the leeks and carrots and continuing cooking, stirring, until the leek is softened, about 8 minutes. Mix in ginger and cook until fragrant, 1 minute longer. Add water and salt and bring to a boil. Reduce heat, cover, and simmer soup until carrots are very tender, about 20 minutes. Let cool a few minutes.

2 Puree the soup in batches in the blender, adding orange juice and maple syrup. Blend each batch for 1 or 2 minutes to get the soup super smooth and creamy. Add additional water or orange juice if the soup seems a bit thick. Return the soup to the pot and heat gently. Season to taste with additional salt, if needed.

PAIR WITH SIDE ON PAGE 79.

SIDE ASIAN CHICKEN SALAD WITH ORANGE AND EDAMAME

This salad is light and refreshing, with lots of healthy vegetables, juicy slices of chicken, and a citrus-based dressing.

SERVES 4

SALAD:

3 boneless skinless chicken breast halves, tenderloins removed and set aside

1/4 teaspoon salt

1 tablespoon extra-virgin olive oil

1/2 cup unsalted cashews

1 cup frozen, shelled edamame beans

1 head of butterhead or Bibb lettuce or baby greens (about 6 cups)

1 cup bite-size pieces frisée (if available)

2 stalks celery, peeled, halved lengthwise, and very thinly sliced

2 navel oranges, cut into sections (see page 34)

1/2 small red onion, very thinly sliced

DRESSING:

2 tablespoons freshly squeezed lime juice

1/4 cup freshly squeezed orange juice

1 tablespoon Dijon mustard

6 tablespoons canola oil

1 teaspoon honey

1/2 teaspoon Asian chili sauce or Sriracha sauce

1/2 teaspoon kosher salt

1 Preheat the oven to 350°. Preheat a heavy or thick-bottomed skillet for several minutes over medium heat. Cover the chicken pieces with plastic wrap and pound with a small skillet or meat pounder until the pieces are even in thickness. Season with salt. Add the oil to the pan and sauté the chicken breasts 4 to 5 minutes on each side until chicken is just cooked, 160˚ on an instant-read thermometer. When cool enough to handle, thinly slice chicken on the diagonal.

2 Place the cashews on a baking sheet and toast until golden, 6 to 7 minutes.

3 Bring a small pot of water to a boil and cook the edamame for 3 minutes. Drain and run under cold water to stop the cooking and keep them bright green.

4 Combine the lettuce, frisée if available, celery, orange segments, red onion, and edamame in a wide bowl or platter.

5 Combine the dressing ingredients in a blender or whisk until creamy. Use a piece of lettuce to taste the dressing and make any adjustments needed. To serve, place sliced chicken on top of the salad, sprinkle with nuts, and pass the dressing on the side.

PAIR WITH SOUP ON PAGE 77.

POULTRY

SOUP CHICKEN VEGETABLE SOUP WITH FARRO

Similar to a chicken barley soup, this recipe uses a nice, chewy grain called farro instead of barley. The porcini mushrooms add a lot of flavor. For the chicken, use any leftover chicken or roast two split chicken breasts while the soup is cooking.

SERVES 6 TO 8

1 ounce dried porcini mushrooms

4 1/2 cups hot water

1 onion, diced

1 whole leek, trimmed, cut in half lengthwise, rinsed, and thinly sliced

2 tablespoons extra-virgin olive oil

2 cloves garlic, finely minced

1/2 cup white wine (optional)

4 cups chicken stock

3 medium carrots, peeled and diced

2 stalks celery, diced

2 parsnips, peeled and diced

1/2 cup farro, rinsed, or 1/2 cup barley, rinsed

2 teaspoons fresh thyme leaves, or 1/2 teaspoon dried thyme

4 tablespoons minced fresh parsley

1 to 2 teaspoons kosher salt

1 (14-ounce) can diced tomatoes, with juices

1 1/2 cups diced cooked chicken (see page 39 for a quick method for cooking chicken)

1 In a small bowl, soak the porcini mushrooms in about 2 1/2 cups of hot tap water for at least 15 minutes. Drain the mushrooms in a fine sieve, reserving 2 cups of the soaking water to add to the soup. Remove the mushrooms, mince, and set aside.

2 In a soup pot, sauté the onion and leek in the olive oil over medium-high heat until soft, about 6 minutes. Add garlic and sauté another 1 or 2 minutes. Add the wine and simmer for 1 or 2 minutes, then add the chicken stock, 2 cups water, 2 cups mushroom-soaking water (8 cups of liquid total), chopped porcini, carrots, celery, parsnips, farro or barley, thyme, 1 tablespoon parsley, 1 teaspoon salt, and the diced tomatoes plus their juices. Bring to a boil, reduce heat to medium-low, and simmer, covered, until the farro or barley is tender, 30 to 35 minutes for farro, 50 to 55 minutes for barley.

3 Stir in the cooked chicken; taste and add additional salt. Ladle into bowls and garnish with the remaining minced parsley.

SIDE CRISPY ROMAINE SALAD WITH CROUTONS AND LEMON-PARMESAN DRESSING

The light crunch of romaine and croutons in this Caesar-like salad contrasts beautifully with a slow-cooked soup. You'll have enough dressing to store for another salad.

SERVES 6

CROUTONS:

3 cups French or Italian bread, crusts removed, cubed

1 teaspoon finely minced garlic

2 tablespoons extra-virgin olive oil

Salt and freshly ground black pepper

SALAD:

1 head romaine lettuce (6 to 8 cups), soaked 30 minutes in very cold water to crisp up, and spun dry

1 just-ripe avocado, diced

1 cucumber, peeled, halved lengthwise, and sliced

1/4 red onion, thinly sliced

Parmigiano-Reggiano shavings, to taste

LEMON-PARMESAN DRESSING:

3 tablespoons freshly squeezed lemon juice

1/2 teaspoon minced garlic

1 teaspoon Dijon mustard

1/4 cup grated Parmigiano-Reggiano cheese

1/2 cup extra-virgin olive oil

Salt and freshly ground black pepper

1 To make the croutons, preheat the oven to 350˚. In a medium bowl, mix the bread cubes and the garlic. Drizzle olive oil over the bread and toss with salt and pepper. Place on a baking sheet; bake for 10 to 12 minutes or until croutons are lightly crisp.

2 To make the salad, trim the romaine and chop or tear the leaves into bite-size pieces. Place the lettuce, avocado, cucumber, and red onion in a large bowl.

3 To make the dressing, place the lemon juice, garlic, mustard, cheese, and olive oil in a blender and blend thoroughly. Add salt and pepper to taste.

4 Pour just enough dressing over the salad to coat the greens. Mix gently. Top with the garlic croutons. Using a vegetable peeler, shave slivers of Parmigiano-Reggiano over the top.

`SOUP` CHICKEN AND ESCAROLE SOUP WITH ORZO

Escarole is a pleasantly bitter green that looks like a head of leafy lettuce. I don't know why it makes such a comforting soup, but it does. This recipe provides instruction for roasting split chicken breasts for the chicken, but using leftover chicken or rotisserie chicken works equally well.

SERVES 6 TO 8

- 2/3 cup uncooked orzo
- Splash of extra-virgin olive oil, plus 3 tablespoons
- 2 split bone-in chicken breasts or 2 cups cooked chicken, shred into bite-size pieces
- 1 teaspoon salt, plus more for orzo and chicken
- 2 medium onions, thinly sliced
- 2 cloves garlic, finely minced
- 8 cups chicken stock (preferably homemade)
- 1 medium head escarole, rinsed and roughly chopped (about 5 cups)
- Grated Parmigiano-Reggiano cheese, to taste

1 Bring a pot of water to a boil. Cook orzo according to package directions, drain, and cool. Add a splash of olive oil to keep orzo from sticking.

2 Preheat the oven to 350°. Rub split chicken breasts with salt and 1 tablespoon olive oil. Place on a baking sheet and roast for 40 to 45 minutes, until just cooked. When chicken is cool enough to handle, remove the meat from the bone and shred by hand into bite-size strips. It's okay if the chicken is slightly undercooked; it will finish cooking in the soup and be very tender.

3 While the chicken is roasting, heat the remaining 2 tablespoons oil in a heavy-bottomed soup pot over medium-high heat. Sauté the onions until golden and almost caramelized, 12 to 15 minutes, stirring often and scraping the bottom of the pot to prevent sticking. As the onions shed their moisture, gradually reduce the heat to low to prevent burning. Add the garlic and cook 1 or 2 additional minutes, stirring constantly.

4 Add the chicken stock and bring to a boil. Add 1 teaspoon salt and the escarole, reduce heat and simmer, partially covered, until the escarole is tender, about 10 minutes. Just before serving, add the shredded chicken and cooked orzo and heat gently. Taste, and add salt if needed. Serve hot with a generous sprinkling of the Parmesan cheese in each bowl.

SIDE BUTTERMILK BISCUITS

These are best warm from the oven.

MAKES 9 (3-INCH) BISCUITS

2 1/2 cups all-purpose flour, plus more for dusting

2 teaspoons baking powder

1/2 teaspoon baking soda

1/4 teaspoon salt

2 teaspoons sugar

8 tablespoons (1 stick) unsalted butter, cold

1 cup buttermilk

1 egg

2 tablespoons milk, half-and-half, or cream

1 Preheat the oven to 425°. In the bowl of a food processor, place the flour, baking powder, baking soda, salt, and sugar. Mix to incorporate.

2 Cut butter into small cubes and add to the flour mixture. Pulse until mixture resembles coarse crumbs or pebbles. Transfer mixture to a bowl.

3 Add the buttermilk and mix lightly until dough begins to come together. The dough will be thick, not overly moist, but if the mixture seems a bit too dry and doesn't come together, add a bit more buttermilk. Do not overmix.

4 Pat or roll out the dough on a floured work surface into a square about 3/4 inch thick. Use a 3-inch biscuit cutter to cut the biscuits, or cut into even sections with a knife. Gather the dough scraps and reuse.

5 Combine the egg and milk in a small bowl. Brush egg wash on tops of biscuits.

6 Bake until golden brown, 15 to 18 minutes. Serve immediately.

SOUP **CHICKEN TORTILLA SOUP**

This chunky chicken soup flavored with cumin, chili, and lime is served with a variety of toppings that include avocado, fresh cilantro, and crisp tortilla strips. Paired with a festive quinoa salad, it makes a nice combination for a casual dinner party. Everything can be prepared ahead of time and passed at the table.

SERVES 6

3 split bone-in skin-on chicken breasts

3 tablespoons extra-virgin olive oil

Salt

12 (6- or 7-inch) corn tortillas

1 whole leek, trimmed, cut in half lengthwise, rinsed, and sliced

2 cloves garlic, finely minced

1 jalapeño pepper, seeded and finely minced

2 teaspoons chili powder

1 teaspoon ground cumin

8 cups chicken stock

1 (28-ounce) can diced tomatoes, drained

Kernels from 2 ears fresh corn (about 1 cup)

1 cup chopped cilantro, for topping

2 ripe but firm avocadoes, diced, for topping

Shredded Monterey jack or cheddar cheese, for topping

2 limes, cut into wedges, for topping

1 Preheat the oven to 350°. Rub chicken breasts with 1 tablespoon olive oil and sprinkle with salt. Place on a baking sheet and roast until just cooked, 40 to 45 minutes. Ideally, the chicken will be slightly undercooked, and finish cooking in the soup for optimal tenderness. When chicken is cool enough to handle, shred by hand into strips. Leave the oven on.

2 Cut tortillas in half, and then cut each half into 1/4-inch strips. Place on a baking sheet and drizzle with 1 tablespoon of the olive oil and a sprinkling of salt. Mix with tongs. Bake until lightly crispy, turning occasionally with tongs, 10 to 12 minutes. Set aside until ready to serve.

3 In a soup pot, over medium-low heat, sauté the leek, garlic, and jalapeño in the remaining 1 tablespoon olive oil for 1 to 2 minutes, stirring often. Stir in the chili powder and cumin and continue stirring until fragrant, about 30 seconds.

4 Add stock, tomatoes, and 1 teaspoon salt and bring to a boil. Reduce heat to low and simmer soup for 10 minutes, covered. Add the corn and simmer for an additional 5 minutes. Just before serving, add the chicken, heat gently, and adjust the seasonings.

5 Arrange the tortilla strips and other toppings on a platter. Ladle the soup into bowls and pass the cilantro, avocadoes, cheese, and lime wedges (don't skip the lime juice, it enlivens the soup).

PAIR WITH SIDE ON PAGE 88.

SIDE MEXICAN QUINOA SALAD WITH BLACK BEANS, CORN, AND EDAMAME

Edamame, or fresh soybeans, aren't usually found in Mexican dishes, but they are a welcome addition. You can be flexible with the dressing: If you don't have cumin, just use chili powder or try adding a bit of cayenne for additional heat if you like it spicy. Dress the salad just before serving. The quinoa will absorb dressing as it sits, so you can add more lime juice as desired. This recipe makes enough for a crowd and can easily be cut in half.

SERVES 8

1 1/2 cups quinoa, rinsed well and drained

2 1/4 cups water

1/2 teaspoon salt

1 cup frozen shelled edamame beans

Kernels from 2 ears fresh corn (about 1 cup)

1 red bell pepper, roasted, peeled, and diced (see page 34)

1 cup canned black beans, rinsed in hot water

1/2 to 1 cup cilantro leaves, washed well, spun dry, and loosely chopped

DRESSING:

6 tablespoons freshly squeezed lime juice

6 tablespoons extra-virgin olive oil

1 clove garlic, finely minced

1/2 teaspoon chili powder

1/2 teaspoon ground cumin

3/4 teaspoon kosher salt, or to taste

1 Place the quinoa, water, and 1/2 teaspoon salt in a saucepan. Bring to a boil, reduce heat, cover, and cook on low for 13 to 15 minutes, until water is absorbed. Turn off heat and let rest for 10 minutes. Fluff with a fork, add to a large bowl, and cool to room temperature.

2 Bring another saucepan full of water to a boil. Add edamame and boil for 2 minutes and then add the corn, and continue boiling for 2 minutes longer. Drain the edamame and corn and run under cold water to stop the cooking and keep the color. Add corn, edamame, red pepper, and black beans to the quinoa.

3 For the dressing, whisk together the lime juice, olive oil, garlic, chili powder, cumin, and salt in a small bowl. When ready to serve, pour dressing over quinoa and vegetables and toss gently to combine. Add cilantro and mix gently. Taste and add more salt and lime if necessary. Serve at room temperature.

PAIR WITH SOUP ON PAGE 87.

SOUP GREEK-STYLE CHICKEN AND ORZO SOUP

Avgolemono is the Greek version of Mom's homemade chicken soup. It's typically a simple soup of chicken broth and rice, enriched and smoothly thickened with eggs and lemon. I expanded on that idea to include diced chicken, carrots, spinach, and orzo pasta. Serve this accompanied by fattoush—a crunchy Middle Eastern salad of romaine, fresh herbs, feta cheese, and baked pita croutons.

SERVES 6 TO 8

2/3 cup uncooked orzo

Olive oil

7 cups chicken stock (preferably homemade)

1 whole leek, trimmed, cut in half lengthwise, rinsed, and sliced

4 carrots, peeled and diced

1 1/2 teaspoons grated lemon zest

1 teaspoon kosher salt

1/4 cup freshly squeezed lemon juice

2 eggs

2 egg yolks

5 to 10 ounces baby spinach, rinsed and chopped

2 cups cooked, diced chicken (see page 39 for cooking chicken, if needed)

1 Bring a pot of water to a boil. Cook orzo according to package directions. Drain and cool. Add a splash of olive oil to keep orzo from sticking together.

2 In a soup pot, bring the stock, leek, carrots, and zest to a boil. Reduce heat to low, cover, and simmer for about 12 minutes, until the leeks and carrots are cooked.

3 In a medium bowl, whisk the lemon juice, eggs, and yolks together until smooth. Into this bowl, slowly and gradually whisk in 2 cups of the hot broth to temper the eggs and prevent them from scrambling. Stir the tempered egg-broth mixture to the soup pot. Cook over medium-low heat, stirring, until slightly thickened, 2 to 3 minutes. The soup should be pale yellow, with a smooth and creamy consistency.

4 Wilt the spinach in a covered skillet over medium heat; add a bit of water if needed to keep spinach from sticking. Add the spinach to the soup, along with the chicken and cooked orzo. Heat gently, 2 to 3 minutes. Taste to see if more salt is needed. Avoid vigorously simmering or boiling the soup, or even prolonged reheating, to keep the best consistency and to keep the chicken tender. If you plan to have soup left over, keep the orzo on the side and add when reheating.

SIDE FATTOUSH SALAD WITH CHICKPEAS AND FETA

The word fattoush means "moistened bread." Of Syrian or Lebanese origin, fattoush salads are a wonderful combination of vegetables, fresh herbs, and toasted pita bread. I've added chickpeas for extra protein. Don't skip this side—it would also go great with any of the lentil or other soups.

SERVES 6

2 (8-inch) pita breads

1 tablespoon extra-virgin olive oil

1 head romaine lettuce, or 2 romaine hearts, chopped into bite-size pieces (about 6 cups)

2 large cucumbers, peeled, seeded, and diced

1/2 red onion, very thinly sliced

2 cups cherry tomatoes, quartered

1 cup cooked chickpeas from a can, rinsed well under hot water (optional)

1/4 cup minced fresh parsley

1/4 cup slivered fresh mint

1 cup sheep's milk feta cheese, crumbled or diced

DRESSING:

1/3 cup freshly squeezed lemon juice

1/3 cup extra-virgin olive oil

1 clove garlic, minced

1 teaspoon ground cumin

1/2 teaspoon kosher salt

Freshly ground black pepper

1 Preheat the oven to 350°. Separate the pitas into 2 layers each and place on a baking sheet. Brush each piece with oil. Bake until lightly crisp, 8 to 10 minutes. When the pita pieces have cooled, break into bite-size pieces. Set aside.

2 In a large bowl or platter, combine the lettuce, cucumber, red onion, tomatoes, chickpeas, parsley, and mint.

3 To prepare the dressing, in a small bowl, whisk together the lemon juice, olive oil, garlic, cumin, salt, and pepper.

4 Just before serving, add the dressing to the salad and toss. Top with the toasted pita (like croutons) and feta cheese.

SOUP YUCATAN CHICKEN AND TOMATILLO SOPA

Martha's Vineyard caterer Jan Buhrman has visited Mexico five times over the years and has consistently searched for the quintessential tortilla soup. "I love going out to the markets and gathering produce and ingredients, inspired by what is available," says Jan. "I love the range of peppers readily available, both dried and fresh. The colors are as brilliant as the clothing the vendors wear at the markets." This soup can be simple with just chicken stock, lime, and cilantro or luxurious if you include squash blossoms, chicharrones, or avocados. The key is to start with a homemade chicken stock.

SERVES 6 TO 8

6 tablespoons extra-virgin olive oil

1 medium onion, diced small

4 cloves garlic, minced

14 to 16 tomatillos, husks removed and discarded, cored, and roughly chopped

8 cups chicken stock (preferably homemade)

5 (5-inch) corn tortillas, cut into 1/2-inch strips

2 poblano peppers, roasted and peeled, or dried peppers like chiles pasillas, seeded and deveined (see page 34)

1/2 bunch cilantro, chopped

2 cups shredded chicken (see page 39 for cooking)

1 or 2 avocadoes, diced

2 large limes, cut into wedges, for garnish

Queso fresco or feta cheese, crumbled, for garnish

1 Heat 4 tablespoons of the oil in a skillet over medium heat. Add the onion and garlic and sauté until lightly browned, about 6 minutes. Add tomatillos and cook for 6 to 7 minutes. Remove to a blender and process until smooth.

2 Place stock in a soup pot and add tomatillo mixture; heat over medium heat for 20 minutes.

3 Meanwhile, heat the remaining 2 tablespoons oil in a medium skillet over medium heat; add the tortilla strips, and cook, turning, until they are crisp, 6 to 8 minutes. Remove tortillas, and set aside for garnish. Keep the skillet on the heat.

4 Slice the peppers into thin strips and add to the hot pan. Toss around for a few minutes to bring out the flavors. Remove from heat.

5 Set out the soup bowls. To each bowl, add some tortilla strips, peppers, cilantro, chicken, and avocado.

6 Just before serving, ladle the hot tomatillo broth into bowls. Limes should be squeezed over the soup just before eating. Top with the queso fresco or feta.

PAIR WITH SIDE ON PAGE 94.

SIDE GARDEN VEGETABLE QUESADILLAS

You can fill these quesadillas with the roasted vegetables and cheese mixture, or if you don't have the time to roast the vegetables, just proceed with the cheese base.

SERVES 6

1 cup diced red or sweet onion

2 cups 1/2-inch-diced zucchini

1 1/2 cups peeled, 1/2-inch-diced eggplant

1/2 cup diced red bell pepper

3 tablespoons extra-virgin olive oil

Salt

2 cups shredded cheddar, Monterey Jack, or fontina cheese, or a mix

2 tablespoons chopped canned chiles

2 tablespoons chopped fresh cilantro

1 teaspoon ground cumin

1 teaspoon chili powder

6 (8- or 9-inch) flour tortillas

1 Preheat the oven to 400°. Place the onion, zucchini, eggplant, and red pepper on a baking sheet. Sprinkle 2 tablespoons olive oil and salt to taste over the vegetables and mix well with your hands. Bake until vegetables are tender, 20 to 25 minutes, stirring once. Set aside to cool.

2 In a bowl, combine the cheese, chiles, cilantro, cumin, and chili powder. Mix well.

3 Mix the cooled vegetables with the cheese. Place about 1/2 cup of the mixture on one side of each tortilla, closer to the center than the edges, and fold over.

4 Heat 1 teaspoon olive oil in a skillet over medium heat and add 2 folded quesadillas, if they fit. Cook until the bottom on one side is slightly golden. Flip over to the other side and cook until cheese is just melted, 4 to 5 minutes. Repeat with the remaining quesadillas, adding more oil for each batch. Cut each quesadilla into 2 or 3 pieces to serve.

PAIR WITH SOUP ON PAGE 92.

SOUP CHICKEN NOODLE SOUP

You can make chicken noodle soup very quickly with frozen homemade chicken stock. If you don't have the stock, see the recipe on page 36 to make chicken stock from scratch. Cook the noodles on the side if you don't plan to consume all the soup immediately, otherwise they'll absorb the broth and become too soft.

SERVES 6 TO 8

8 cups chicken stock (preferably homemade)

1 whole leek, trimmed, cut in half lengthwise, rinsed, and thinly sliced

3 medium carrots, peeled and diced

2 to 3 stalks celery, diced

2 sprigs fresh thyme

2 ounces egg noodles or pasta (about 2 cups)

2 cups diced cooked chicken

2 tablespoons chopped fresh dill or parsley

Salt and freshly ground black pepper

1 Bring the stock to a boil, add the leek, carrots, celery, and thyme sprigs. Reduce the heat, partially cover, and simmer for about 15 minutes. Remove the thyme sprigs.

2 Stir in the noodles and cook until just tender (use the package directions for an estimate on timing).

3 Add the chicken, dill, and salt and pepper to taste.

SIDE DEVILED EGGS

SERVES 4 TO 6

4 eggs

1/4 cup mayonnaise

1 tablespoon chopped fresh chives

Salt

Pinch of cayenne

1 Place eggs in a medium saucepan and fill with enough cold water to cover the eggs by 2 inches. Bring to a boil. Turn off the heat, cover, and let eggs remain in pan for 10 minutes. Remove the eggs and place them in a bowl of cold water to cool before removing the shells.

2 Carefully slice the eggs in half lengthwise. Remove the yolks and place in a small bowl. Mash well with a fork and mix in the mayonnaise, chives, salt to taste, and a pinch of cayenne. Mix until smooth.

3 Place filling in a pastry bag and pipe back into the egg white halves.

SOUP BLACK BEAN AND ROASTED SWEET POTATO SOUP WITH CHICKEN

Black beans cooked from scratch have a wonderful, earthy flavor not found in canned beans. Mix them with sweet potatoes roasted in the oven and diced chicken, and you've got a great soup. If the bit of extra effort it takes to cook the beans seems too much, just remember, you get a tremendous nutritional payoff in return: protein, calcium, iron, fiber, potassium, magnesium, folic acid, and complex carbohydrates for energy. You can freeze any leftovers. For a little something extra, top with cheddar cheese and/or slices of avocado.

SERVES 8 TO 10

1 pound dried black beans, soaked in water overnight and drained

1 dried chipotle pepper

13 to 14 cups water

2 sweet potatoes, peeled and cut into 3/4-inch chunks

3 tablespoons extra-virgin olive oil

2 tablespoons plus 1/2 teaspoon ancho chili powder or chili powder

2 1/2 teaspoons ground cumin

1/2 teaspoon ground coriander

1 1/2 teaspoons kosher salt

2 split bone-in skin-on chicken breasts

2 onions, diced

2 red bell peppers, diced

1 jalapeño pepper, finely minced

3 cloves garlic, finely minced

2 teaspoons dried oregano

1 (28-ounce) can diced tomatoes with juice

1/2 cup chopped fresh cilantro leaves

3 tablespoons freshly squeezed orange juice

1 to 2 tablespoons freshly squeezed lime juice

1 Preheat the oven to 350°. Place the beans, chipotle pepper, and water in a large soup pot. Bring to a boil, reduce heat, and simmer, partially covered, for 1 hour.

2 Meanwhile, place the diced sweet potato on a baking sheet, coat with 1 tablespoon olive oil and sprinkle with 1/2 teaspoon each of chili powder, cumin, coriander, and salt. Roast, turning several times, until the sweet potatoes are just tender, 30 to 35 minutes. Set aside.

3 Rub split chicken breasts with salt and 1 tablespoon olive oil. Place on a baking sheet and roast until just cooked, 35 to 40 minutes. When chicken is cool enough to handle, remove the meat from the bone and shred by hand into bite-size strips.

4 Add the remaining 1 tablespoon oil to a skillet over medium heat and sauté the onions for 8 minutes. Add the red bell pepper and jalapeño pepper and sauté an additional 4 minutes. Then add garlic, the remaining 2 tablespoons chili powder, 2 teaspoons cumin, and the oregano. When the beans in the soup have cooked about 1 hour, add the onion-pepper mixture along with diced tomatoes, half the cilantro, and 1 teaspoon salt. Bring to a boil, then simmer again, partially covered, for an additional 30 minutes.

5 When the soup is done, remove the dried chipotle pepper and add in the sweet potato, chicken, remaining cilantro, orange juice, and lime juice. Heat gently and test for salt.

SIDE CARROT SLAW

A bright side for an earthy soup. You can quickly shred the carrots using the shredding attachment to your food processor.

SERVES 6 TO 8

3 cups peeled and shredded carrots

2 stalks celery, cut in half lengthwise and very thinly sliced on a diagonal

1 1/2 cups thinly sliced green cabbage

1 1/2 cups thinly sliced fresh fennel (optional)

1/4 cup finely minced parsley

DRESSING:

1/2 cup freshly squeezed orange juice

1 tablespoon minced shallot (optional)

2 teaspoons ground cumin

1 tablespoon freshly squeezed lemon juice

2 teaspoons maple syrup or honey

2 tablespoons canola oil

2 tablespoons extra-virgin olive oil

1/2 teaspoon kosher salt, or to taste

1 In a medium bowl, combine carrots, celery, cabbage, fennel, and parsley. Mix gently.

2 For the dressing, in a small bowl, whisk together the orange juice, shallots, cumin, lemon juice, maple syrup or honey, oils, and salt to taste. Just before serving, pour over the salad. Toss, taste, and adjust seasonings.

SOUP ASIAN CHICKEN NOODLE SOUP

You can approach this soup in two ways: You can make a chicken soup from scratch and start at step one. Or, if you already have chicken broth and cooked chicken, you can get the soup done much quicker by prepping your vegetables and starting at step four. Either way, though a bit involved, it's a soup you don't want to miss. Feel free to vary the vegetables, and especially the noodles, according to your likes and dislikes. Don't forget to squeeze in the lime at the end—it subtly changes the flavor.

SERVES 6

1 large leek

1 whole chicken (2 1/2 to 3 pounds), rinsed

12 cups water

Fresh ginger (enough for 1 tablespoon finely grated)

2 stalks lemongrass

1 carrot

1 1/2 cups shiitake mushrooms

2 heads baby bok choy or snow peas or another green vegetable (roughly 2 cups sliced)

1 Cut off the green end of the leek and place it in a soup pot with the chicken and the water and bring to a boil. Turn heat to low, partially cover, and skim off any impurities (foam) that rise to the top. Simmer gently, partially covered (do not boil).

2 While the stock is cooking, prep the vegetables, saving the scraps for the stock: Cut the rest of the leek lengthwise, rinse, and slice. Peel the ginger and grate 1 tablespoon of the inner root. Strip the outer leaves from the lemongrass and mince the very inner leaves near the base for 1 tablespoon. Peel the carrot and cut it into matchsticks; slice the mushrooms; slice the bok choy or string the snow peas. Add scraps of ginger, outer lemongrass leaves, mushroom stems, outer leek leaves, and snow pea strings to the soup pot as you go.

3 When the stock has simmered 50 to 60 minutes, remove the whole chicken to a plate; when it's cool enough to handle remove the meat in large pieces. Place chicken bones back into the pot and continue simmering for another 30 minutes. Shred the chicken meat and refrigerate. Strain the stock, discarding the solids. Set 8 to 10 cups of stock aside for the soup and freeze the rest.

1 (8-ounce) package of noodles, such as fresh Chinese noodles, ramen, udon, or your favorite Asian noodle

2 tablespoons toasted sesame oil or canola oil

2 tablespoons soy sauce

1/2 teaspoon Sriracha or other hot sauce

1 tablespoon rice vinegar

Salt

2 scallions, green part only, thinly sliced

1/3 cup slivered fresh cilantro (optional)

2 limes, quartered

4 Cook the noodles al dente in a large pot of salted water according to package directions, minus 1 to 2 minutes. Drain, drizzle with 1 tablespoon of the sesame oil to keep them separate, and shake strainer until all the steam has been released so noodles don't continue to cook or get sticky. Set aside.

5 In the soup pot, heat the remaining tablespoon oil and sauté the leek, ginger, lemongrass, and sliced mushrooms 3 to 4 minutes, until mushrooms begin to cook. Add 8 cups stock and bring to a boil. Reduce the heat and simmer, partially covered, for 10 minutes. Season with the soy sauce, Sriracha, and a few pinches of salt to taste. Reduce heat to low and add the carrots, bok choy, and desired amount of shredded chicken, and serve immediately. Place the noodles into bowls and ladle the soup over the noodles. Place the scallions, cilantro (if using), and wedges of lime on a plate to pass around the table.

PAIR WITH SIDE ON PAGE 101.

SIDE VEGETARIAN EGG ROLLS

Egg rolls are quite easy to make; finding a package of Asian egg roll wrappers may be the toughest part. I like sautéing the egg rolls in a small amount of oil (or even baking them in the oven without any oil) rather than deep-frying, and serving them with a dipping sauce.

MAKES 12 EGG ROLLS

2 tablespoons canola or peanut oil

3 scallions, white and green parts, thinly sliced

1 tablespoon finely minced fresh ginger

1 cup shredded carrots

5 cups thinly sliced Napa cabbage

2 cups mung bean sprouts (if available)

1 to 2 tablespoons soy sauce

1 package spring roll shells*, thawed

Sweet chili sauce or Asian dumpling sauce such as Maesri brand

1 In a large sauté pan, heat 1 tablespoon oil over low heat and sauté scallions and ginger, 1 to 2 minutes. Turn the heat to medium-high and add shredded carrots, Napa cabbage, and mung bean sprouts; sauté until cabbage is just slightly wilted, 2 to 3 minutes.

2 Add soy sauce to taste and transfer mixture to a colander set over a bowl. Let cool and drain, 7 to 10 minutes.

3 Place 3 or 4 tablespoons of filling toward the bottom of a wrapper and roll upward once, then fold the sides over the filling and continue rolling. Continue with the remaining wrappers and filling. Place on a plate and cover with plastic wrap while you roll the rest. The egg rolls should be cooked within 1 to 2 hours of rolling.

4 Heat the remaining 1 tablespoon oil in a large, heavy skillet over medium heat and sauté the egg rolls in 2 batches, turning so each side becomes golden, about 7 to 8 minutes. Repeat for the remaining egg rolls. Place on paper towels to absorb any excess oil. Serve hot with sweet chili dipping sauce in individual dipping bowls, if possible.

* Wei-chuan spring roll shells, in a red and yellow package, are typically found in the frozen section in Asian grocery stores. Some supermarkets, such as Whole Foods, do sell egg roll wrappers in the refrigerator section, usually near the tofu. These can be a bit thicker (meant for deep frying), but they work in a pinch.

PAIR WITH SOUP ON PAGE 98.

`SOUP` TURKEY NOODLE SOUP

There's always a great opportunity to make a nice big batch of turkey stock after Thanksgiving, stretching your dollar further. You can use some of the stock for turkey noodle soup and freeze the rest for any soup that calls for chicken stock. For a variation, substitute 1 1/2 to 2 cups cooked rice or wild rice for the pasta.

SERVES 8 TO 10

TURKEY STOCK:

1 cooked turkey, meat removed and reserved

1/2 cup white wine

2 onions, chopped

2 stalks celery, chopped

8 to 10 sprigs parsley

TURKEY SOUP:

8 cups turkey stock

1 whole leek, trimmed, cut in half lengthwise, rinsed, and sliced

3 medium carrots, peeled and diced

2 stalks celery, diced, plus any celery leaves, chopped

2 teaspoons chopped fresh thyme leaves

8 fresh sage leaves, minced (optional)

2 tablespoons minced fresh parsley

4 to 6 ounces thin egg noodles*

2 cups shredded or diced cooked turkey meat

1 to 2 teaspoons salt

Freshly ground black pepper

1 To make the turkey stock, place turkey carcass, wine, onions, celery, and parsley in a large stockpot and add water to cover by 2 or 3 inches. Bring to a boil and skim off any impurities (foam) that rise to the top. Lower heat to medium-low, cover partially, and simmer until broth is golden and fully flavored, 3 to 4 hours. Strain liquid into 2 bowls, so it can cool more quickly. Discard solids. After cooling slightly, refrigerate. Before using, skim off any fat that has risen to the top. Freeze whatever you are not going to use right away.

2 To make the soup, bring 8 cups turkey stock to a boil in a soup pot. Add the leek, carrots, celery and chopped celery leaves, thyme, sage, and parsley. Turn heat to low and simmer, partially covered, 15 minutes.

3 Add the noodles and cook until almost done. Add the turkey, season with salt and pepper, and heat gently.

* Pennsylvania Dutch is a nice brand of egg noodles, cut into small pieces and ultra thin—perfect for turkey and chicken soup. You can add the noodles right to the soup, or you can cook them on the side and add when serving so the pasta doesn't swell when reheated.

SIDE DELICATA SQUASH STUFFED WITH APPLES, CRANBERRIES, AND WALNUTS

Delicata squash is an oblong squash, maybe 6 to 8 inches long, streaked with green lines. It is one of the fastest cooking (and best tasting) of the fall squashes. It makes a perfect vehicle for stuffing, as below, or just served with pumpkin pie spices and a sweetener like maple syrup or brown sugar. You can substitute acorn squash if delicata is unavailable, but it needs to be cooked much longer.

SERVES 6

3 delicata squash, cut in half lengthwise and seeded (choose squash of equal sizes)

2 tablespoons butter

3 apples, peeled and thinly sliced (such as Granny Smith)

3 tablespoons dried cranberries or raisins

Salt

1/3 cup toasted walnuts, roughly chopped

Cinnamon, to taste

Maple syrup, to taste

1 Preheat the oven to 350°. Line a large baking pan with parchment paper. Place squash cut side down in prepared baking pan. Bake squash until easily pierced with a fork, about 20 minutes. Be careful not to overcook, or squash will collapse.

2 Meanwhile, melt the butter in a medium skillet over medium-high heat. Add apple slices and cook until soft, but not mushy, 8 to 10 minutes. Mix in the brown sugar until dissolved and remove from heat. Add the cranberries and set aside.

3 Remove squash from oven. Turn over and dab a little butter on the inside of each, spreading evenly. Sprinkle a pinch of salt over each squash.

4 Fill each squash with apples and cranberries. Sprinkle with chopped walnuts. Dust with cinnamon and drizzle a little maple syrup (to taste) over each. Serve immediately, or cover with foil and reheat later (still covered with foil), about 20 minutes at 350°.

VARIATION: For spiced delicata, when squash comes out of the oven, add a dab of butter, some salt, a sprinkle of cinnamon, and a dash of freshly grated nutmeg. Drizzle with light brown sugar or maple syrup.

MEAT

SOUP HARIRA LAMB AND CHICKPEA SOUP

Harira is a traditional Moroccan soup full of spices, lamb, vegetables, and beans or lentils, usually consumed at the end of the Muslim holy month of Ramadan. There are many variations, but this wonderful adaptation is from Martha's Vineyard resident Geraldine Brooks, a former foreign news correspondent who spent time reporting in Africa and the Middle East and a Pulitzer Prize–winning author of three novels, including *People of the Book*. Don't leave out the broken pasta at the end, it really adds to the soup.

SERVES 6

1 1/2 to 2 pounds lamb from shoulder or leg, cut into 3/4- to 1-inch cubes, fat trimmed and discarded

Salt and freshly ground black pepper

2 tablespoons extra-virgin olive oil, plus a splash

2 medium onions, diced

4 medium to large carrots, peeled and diced

2 cloves garlic, minced

2 teaspoons finely grated fresh ginger

1 1/2 teaspoons ground cumin

1 1/2 teaspoons turmeric

1 1/2 teaspoons ground coriander

1 cinnamon stick or 1/2 teaspoon ground cinnamon

1/2 teaspoon cardamom

1/2 teaspoon paprika

6 cups water

1 (28-ounce) can diced tomatoes with juices

1 1/2 cups cooked chickpeas or 1 (15-ounce) can, rinsed

1 fresh Scotch bonnet pepper, minced

4 to 6 ounces vermicelli or angel-hair pasta, broken into small pieces

3 tablespoons chopped fresh cilantro

3 tablespoons chopped fresh parsley

2 to 4 tablespoons chopped fresh mint

1 Season the lamb cubes with salt and pepper. In a large soup pot, heat 1 tablespoon oil over medium-high heat and brown the lamb in 2 batches, using a spatula to turn the pieces to brown on several sides, about 4 minutes. Remove meat from pot and set aside.

2 Add the remaining tablespoon of oil to the pot and sauté the onions and carrots over medium heat, 6 to 8 minutes. Add the garlic, ginger, cumin, turmeric, coriander, cinnamon, cardamom, and paprika and sauté, 1 to 2 minutes.

3 Add the meat back into the pot, add the water, and bring to a boil. Lower heat to a low simmer, cover, and simmer (do not boil), 1 hour.

4 Skim off any fat that rises to the surface and add the tomato, chickpeas, Scotch bonnet pepper, and salt and pepper to taste. Simmer until the lamb is fork-tender, 20 to 30 minutes.

5 While the soup is finishing, bring a small pot of salted water to boil and cook the pasta pieces until al dente. Drain and shake until all the steam has been released. Add a splash of olive oil and set aside.

6 Just before serving the soup, mix in the fresh herbs and taste for salt and pepper. Place a handful of pasta in each bowl, ladle in the soup, and serve.

SIDE MEZZE

Harira is a great party soup, especially if you ask your friends to bring small plates to share based on Middle Eastern foods. If everyone brings one side dish, you will have a true feast.

Here are some ideas:
Hummus and pita chips
Spinach triangles or spinach pie
Olives
Stuffed grape leaves
Fattoush
Falafels
Kibbeh
Spicy eggplant dip
Carrot salad

`SOUP` BEEF, FARRO, AND VEGETABLE SOUP

This is definitely a meal in a bowl with slow-cooked chuck beef cut into small, melt-in-your-mouth cubes, whole grain farro, and lots of vegetables. Add twice-baked potatoes on the side, for a true winter feast. Using a piece of chuck beef you cut yourself, not the precut "stew" meat which tends to be a mix of cuts, will give you the best tasting and most tender results. It's a bit more time-consuming, but worth the effort. This recipe makes a lot of soup, you may want to freeze your leftovers.

SERVES 8 TO 10

1 (2 1/2- to 3 1/2-pound) piece of chuck roast, cut into approximately 3/4-inch pieces and trimmed of solid fat

1 teaspoon kosher salt, plus more to taste

 Freshly ground black pepper

1 1/2 tablespoons all-purpose flour

2 tablespoons extra-virgin olive oil

1/2 cup red wine

8 cups chicken stock

4 cups water

2 teaspoons Worcestershire sauce

1 large onion, diced

1 whole leek, trimmed, cut in half lengthwise, rinsed, and thinly sliced

4 carrots, peeled and diced

2 stalks celery, diced

2 teaspoons chopped fresh thyme leaves or 1 teaspoon dried thyme

1 (28-ounce) can diced tomatoes with juices

2/3 cup farro, rinsed*

1/2 cup minced fresh parsley

1 cup small-diced green beans

Kernels from 2 ears fresh corn (about 1 cup)

1 Season the beef cubes with salt and pepper and dust lightly with the flour. In a large soup pot, heat 1 tablespoon oil over medium-high heat and brown half of the beef, using a spatula to turn the pieces to brown on several sides, about 4 minutes. Set aside the first batch and brown the second. Add the first batch of meat back into the pot, and add the wine, using a wooden spoon to scrape up flavorful browned bits. Stir in the chicken stock, water, Worcestershire sauce, and onion. Bring to a boil, skimming off any impurities (foam) that rise to the top. Reduce heat to medium-low and add the leek, carrots, celery, and thyme; partially cover, and simmer (do not boil), 40 minutes.

2 Add the tomato, farro, half the parsley, and 1 teaspoon salt. Bring to a boil again, reduce heat, and simmer 15 minutes. Add the green beans and corn and continue cooking until the farro, which has a texture similar to barley, is cooked and the meat is very tender, another 10 to 15 minutes. Skim off any fat that rises to the top as you go or at the end.

3 Add the remaining parsley and season to taste with salt and a few grinds of fresh pepper.

* If farro, an Italian grain, is unavailable, substitute 1/2 cup barley and add when you add the carrots and celery. Cook for a longer time, 45 to 50 minutes. Farro can be found at most Whole Foods Markets, local Italian grocers, or online.

PAIR WITH SIDE ON PAGE 110.

SIDE TWICE-BAKED POTATOES

Twice-baked potatoes work especially well with beef-vegetable soups and can be made ahead of time. You can also vary the fillings.

SERVES 4

4 large Idaho potatoes, scrubbed and pricked with a fork
3 tablespoons butter
Salt
1/3 cup sour cream
1 cup shredded cheddar cheese
2 tablespoons finely chopped fresh chives

1 Preheat the oven to 350°. Place the potatoes directly on the oven rack and bake until soft when poked with a sharp knife, about 1 hour and 15 minutes (check after 1 hour). Let cool slightly.

2 Preheat the oven to 375°. Lay the potatoes on a work surface and slice off the top third of each. Scoop out all but a 1/2-inch border in the potato and remove all of the potato from the tops. Place the potato flesh in a bowl, adding the butter and salt to taste. Put the potato flesh through a potato ricer, or mash or mix with a hand-mixer until creamy.

3 Mix in the sour cream, cheddar cheese, and chives. Season the inside of the potato boats with salt and neatly fill with the potato stuffing.

4 Place filled potatoes on a baking sheet and reheat until very hot and slightly crusty on top, 20 to 30 minutes. If you don't like them crusty, you can also cover with foil for the first half of the reheating.

PAIR WITH SOUP ON PAGE 109.

SOUP MEXICAN BEEF, VEGETABLE, AND QUINOA SOUP

This Mexican-flavored soup has tender, tasty beef cubes, lots of vegetables, and quinoa. Quinoa, a tiny whole grain from South America (pronounced KEEN-wa), packs protein, calcium, and iron and has been a nourishing Peruvian staple for centuries. This is a soup to rev up your reserves in winter.

SERVES 8 TO 10

1 (3-pound) piece of chuck roast, cut into approximately 3/4-inch pieces and trimmed of solid fat

1 teaspoon kosher salt, plus more for seasoning meat

Freshly ground black pepper

1 tablespoon all-purpose flour

1 tablespoon extra-virgin olive oil

1 onion, diced

2 cloves garlic, minced

1 1/2 teaspoons ground cumin

2 teaspoons chili powder

11 cups water

1 whole leek, trimmed, cut in half lengthwise, rinsed, and sliced

2 carrots, peeled and diced

2 stalks celery, diced

1 (28-ounce) can diced tomatoes, with juices

2 to 3 teaspoons chipotle adobo sauce* or 1 jalapeño pepper, minced

1/3 cup quinoa, rinsed

1 cup small-diced green beans

Kernels from 2 ears fresh corn (about 1 cup)

1/2 cup chopped fresh cilantro

1 Season the beef cubes with salt and pepper and dust with flour. In a large soup pot with a thick bottom, heat the oil over medium-high heat and brown half of the beef, using a spatula or tongs to turn the pieces to brown on several sides, about 4 minutes. Set aside the first batch and brown the second. Add the first batch of meat back into the pot; add the onion, garlic, cumin, and chili powder and cook for 2 or 3 minutes, stirring constantly.

2 Add the water, scraping up the brown bits, and bring to a boil, skimming off any impurities (foam) that rise to the top. Add the leek, carrots, celery, and 1 teaspoon salt. Reduce heat to medium-low, partially cover, and simmer (do not boil) until the meat is very tender (easily pierced with a fork and not chewy), about 70 minutes.

3 Add the tomato, 2 teaspoons adobo sauce, quinoa, green beans, and corn. Bring to a boil again, reduce heat, and simmer an additional 10 minutes. Skim off any fat that rises to the top as you go, or at the end.

4 Add the cilantro and season to taste with additional salt, a few grinds of fresh pepper, and another teaspoon of the adobo sauce if you'd like it a bit spicier.

* You can find small cans of chipotle peppers packed in an adobo sauce in the supermarket section with chopped chilies, taco fillings, and other Mexican foods. The peppers are very hot, but the sauce works great to flavor a soup and give it a bit of heat.

SIDE PAPUSAS

Papusas are a thick flatbread found in Latin America made from corn flour known as masa harina. They are prepared with a variety of fillings, including cheese, refried beans, or pork. You can make the batter ahead of time, but it's best to cook the papusas just before serving them with a spoonful of salsa.

SERVES 4 OR MORE AS AN APPETIZER

2 cups masa harina*
1 1/2 to 2 cups water
1 1/4 teaspoons kosher salt
Olive oil or canola oil

FILLING:

1 cup cooked pinto beans
Salt
1/4 cup chopped fresh cilantro
1 1/2 cups shredded cheddar cheese
Salsa

1 In a medium bowl, combine the masa harina, 1 1/2 cups water, and the salt. Mix with a wooden spoon or your hands for 2 to 3 minutes to form a dough. The dough should be smooth and thick, but not sticky. If it is too dry, add a bit more water. If it is sticky, add a bit more masa.

2 To make the filling, combine the beans, salt to taste, and cilantro in a bowl. Put the shredded cheese in another small bowl.

3 To make the papusas, divide the dough into 15 portions. Take one portion in your hand and flatten it slightly into a circle. With your thumb, make a depression in the center to form a cup or bowl. Add 4 or 5 of the beans mixed with cilantro and about 2 tablespoons cheddar cheese. Pinch the edges up over the filling to form a ball again, enclosing the filling. Gently pat the ball back into a disk, about 1/4 inch thick and 4 inches wide, being careful to keep the filling inside. To make this disk you are gradually incorporating the filling into the flattened papusa. Repeat to make the rest of the papusas.

4 Heat a skillet or griddle over medium heat, add a thin coating of oil, and cook the papusas until golden brown, 4 to 5 minutes. Carefully turn over and brown the other side. Serve with salsa on the side.

* Masa harina can be found in most grocery stores in either the Mexican food aisle or with other flours.

SOUP ITALIAN WEDDING SOUP WITH KALE AND MINI MEATBALLS

Mini meatballs are simmered in a chicken broth with mellow greens then topped off with Parmesan cheese. It's a great soup to serve guests. Depending on your level of patience (or the number of helpful hands in the kitchen), you can roll the meatballs very small, up to about an inch in diameter. Baking them in the oven makes the job much quicker.

SERVES 6

MEATBALLS:

3/4 pound ground beef

1/3 cup fresh bread crumbs (made from any bread you have in the house, crumbed in a food processor)

1/4 cup water

1/3 cup grated Parmigiano-Reggiano cheese

1 clove garlic, finely minced

1/2 teaspoon dried oregano

2 tablespoons minced fresh parsley

3/4 teaspoon kosher salt

1/4 teaspoon freshly ground black pepper

SOUP:

2 tablespoons extra-virgin olive oil

1 large onion diced (about 2 cups)

2 stalks celery, cut in half lengthwise and thinly sliced

2 cloves garlic, minced

8 cups chicken stock (preferably homemade)

2 1/2 teaspoons kosher salt

3 cups thinly sliced kale, center ribs removed before slicing

2 cups Savoy cabbage, cored and thinly sliced*

Freshly ground black pepper

Small hunk of Parmigiano-Reggiano cheese

1 Preheat the oven to 375°. To make the meatballs, mix the ground beef, bread crumbs, water, Parmesan cheese, garlic, oregano, parsley, salt, and pepper together in a bowl. Roll into approximately 1-inch balls and place on a baking sheet. Cover and refrigerate.

2 To make the soup, heat the oil in a thick-bottomed soup pot over medium-high heat. Sauté the onions for about 10 minutes, until golden, stirring often and scraping the bottom of the pot to prevent sticking. Add the celery and sauté another 5 minutes. Add the garlic and cook another minute over low heat. Add the chicken stock and 1 teaspoon salt and bring to a boil. Add the kale and Savoy cabbage, lower heat and simmer, covered, about 15 minutes.

3 Meanwhile, bake meatballs for about 12 minutes (they don't brown up as much in the oven as they would sautéed in a pan, but that's okay). Remove from the oven and add to the soup, simmering about 5 minutes to meld flavors.

4 Taste the soup and add more salt and a few grinds of black pepper to taste. Ladle into soup bowls. Garnish with a few shavings Parmigiano-Reggiano cheese (a vegetable peeler works great for this). Pass the cheese and a grater at the table in case people want to add more.

* Savoy cabbage is the crinkly green cabbage, a bit milder than regular green cabbage, which I don't think would be as good in this soup. If Savoy cabbage is not available, replace it with escarole.

VARIATION: Add cheese tortellini to the soup. Keep the kale, but take out the celery and cabbage.

PAIR WITH SIDE ON PAGE 116.

SIDE GARLIC BREAD

SERVES 6

3 tablespoons salted butter

3 tablespoons extra-virgin olive oil

1 large clove garlic, finely minced

1 loaf French, Italian, or sourdough bread, sliced

1 tablespoon minced fresh parsley (optional)

1 Preheat the oven to 350°. Heat the butter, olive oil, and garlic in a small saucepan over low to medium heat until garlic sizzles, 2 to 3 minutes. Make sure the garlic doesn't turn golden or start to burn. Remove from the heat.

2 Using a pastry brush, brush the garlic mixture onto one side of each slice of bread. Sprinkle with a bit of parsley, if desired. Place slices on a large sheet of foil and reshape into a loaf. Wrap tightly in foil and heat in the oven for 10 to 15 minutes, or until very hot.

PAIR WITH SOUP ON PAGE 115.

SOUP BEEF STEW

Make this stew in a large, heavy-bottomed stove-to-oven soup pot, such as a Le Creuset. Cut a chuck roast into cubes for melt-in-your-mouth flavorful beef; if you start with a 3-pound piece, you might end up with about 2 1/2 pounds after the fat is cut out.

SERVES 6

3 pounds beef chuck, trimmed of fat and cut into 1 1/2-inch cubes

Salt and freshly ground black pepper

3 tablespoons extra-virgin olive oil

1 large onion, diced

3 cloves garlic, minced

3 tablespoons all-purpose flour

1 cup red wine

3 tablespoons tomato paste

4 cups chicken stock

1 bay leaf

1 tablespoon Worcestershire sauce

1 teaspoon dried thyme

6 medium red potatoes, peeled and quartered or cut into chunks for roasting

2 cups green beans, cut in halves or thirds

4 large carrots, peeled and sliced on a diagonal

1/4 cup minced fresh parsley leaves

1 Preheat the oven to 350°. Sprinkle the beef with salt and pepper. Heat 2 tablespoons of the oil in a large soup pot over medium-high heat. Brown the beef on all sides in 2 batches. Remove meat from pot and set aside.

2 Add the onion and sauté 4 to 5 minutes. Add the garlic and sauté another minute or so. Sprinkle the flour over the onion and garlic and cook 1 to 2 minutes, stirring often. Add the wine and tomato paste, scraping up any browned bits that may have stuck to pot. Add the stock, bay leaf, Worcestershire sauce, and thyme; bring to a simmer. Add the meat; return to simmer, cover, and put in the oven to cook until the beef is fork-tender, about 1 1/2 hours.

3 Meanwhile, place the potatoes on a baking sheet, and mix with the remaining 1 tablespoon oil; add salt to taste. Roast until tender, about 40 minutes. Place the green beans in the top of a steamer set over simmering water and steam, 4 minutes. Run the beans under cold water to stop the cooking. Steam the carrots 2 to 3 minutes, then run them under cold water.

4 Just before serving, add the potatoes to the stew and reheat gently. Stir in the carrots, green beans, and parsley. Season with additional salt and pepper.

NOTE FROM THE KITCHEN: I like to brown the beef in 2 pots—the soup pot and another large skillet—to get twice the amount of flavorful brown bits left after sautéing. After you remove the meat, scrape the brown bits from the skillet into the soup pot. I usually cook the vegetables on the side to get the best texture and then add them to the stew.

PAIR WITH SIDE ON PAGE 118.

SIDE CHEDDAR-DILL BISCUITS

Warm from the oven, these biscuits could accompany quite a few other soups as well. I've enjoyed them with beef, chicken, and vegetable soups.

MAKES 12 TO 16 BISCUITS, DEPENDING ON THE SIZE OF THE CUTTER

- 3 cups all-purpose flour, plus more for dusting
- 2 1/2 teaspoons baking powder
- 1/2 teaspoon baking soda
- 1 teaspoon salt
- 8 tablespoons (1 stick) unsalted cold butter, cut into small dice
- 2 tablespoons chopped fresh dill or chives or parsley (optional)
- 1 1/2 cups shredded sharp cheddar cheese or pepper-Jack cheese
- 1 to 1 1/4 cups buttermilk

1 Preheat the oven to 400°. Line a baking sheet with parchment paper. Place flour, baking powder, baking soda, and salt in the bowl of a food processor and pulse to combine. Add the diced butter and pulse until the mixture forms small pebbles.

2 Turn the flour mixture into a bowl and add the dill and cheese. Mix in 1 cup buttermilk, then mix in the remaining buttermilk a little at a time.

3 Turn dough out onto another piece of parchment paper; sprinkle a little flour on top to keep your hands from sticking to the dough, and lightly press out with your hands until about 1 inch high. Using a biscuit cutter, cut into rounds. Gather and reuse the scraps. Place the biscuits on the prepared baking sheet and bake until the tops are lightly golden and a toothpick inserted in the center of a biscuit comes out clean, 16 to 20 minutes.

PAIR WITH SOUP ON PAGE 117.

SOUP WONTON SOUP

The pork wontons in this soup are definitely worth the effort: if you have kids around, enlist their help to fill the wontons. If you don't eat pork, try substituting ground dark turkey.

SERVES 6

1 tablespoon canola or vegetable oil

1 whole leek, trimmed, cut in half lengthwise, rinsed, and thinly sliced

1 tablespoon freshly grated ginger

1 1/2 cups sliced shiitake mushrooms

8 cups chicken stock (preferably homemade)

2 cups thinly sliced bok choy or baby bok choy

1 medium carrot, thinly sliced on a diagonal, slices cut into matchsticks

1 to 2 tablespoons soy sauce, to taste

A few drops of Sriracha or other hot sauce, to taste

A few drops of rice vinegar or fresh lime juice, to taste

PORK WONTONS:

1 tablespoon freshly grated ginger

1 tablespoon soy sauce

2 teaspoons rice cooking wine

2 tablespoons finely chopped scallion whites

1 teaspoon toasted sesame oil

2 teaspoons cornstarch

1/2 pound ground pork

1/2 cup grated daikon radish (optional, adds a nice crunch)

25 to 30 wonton wrappers*

1 In a large, wide soup pot over medium-low heat, add the oil and leek and sauté 3 to 4 minutes. Add the ginger and shiitake mushrooms and cook another 2 to 3 minutes, stirring often and scraping the bottom of the pot. Add the chicken stock and bring to a boil. Turn heat to low, cover, and let the soup simmer, 10 minutes. Remove soup from heat while you make the wontons.

2 To make the wontons, in a medium bowl, mix the ginger, soy, rice wine, scallions, sesame oil, and cornstarch together. Add the pork and daikon radish, if using, and mix thoroughly.

3 Lay six wontons wrappers on a clean cutting board. Set a small bowl of water nearby. Using your fingers, moisten all the edges of each wonton. Add 1 heaping teaspoon of the pork filling in the center of each wonton and bring the edges together in the shape of a triangle. Press out any air pockets inside and press edges together firmly to seal. Bring the left and right corners together over the filling. Overlap the tips of these corners, moisten with water, and press to seal. Set aside on a baking sheet lined with parchment paper or dusted with cornstarch. Cover with plastic wrap, and store in the refrigerator until ready to use.

4 Just before serving, return soup to heat and bring to a boil. Gently add the wontons, sliced bok choy, and carrots, and simmer over medium heat for about 6 or 7 minutes, until the filling is cooked. Season the soup to taste with soy sauce, hot sauce, and lime or rice vinegar. Serve immediately.

* Depending on the shape of the wontons (typically a rectangle), I usually cut off a strip 1/4 to 1/3 of an inch wide, so the wontons are square and easily fold over to create a triangle. Don't cook the wontons in the soup before you are ready to eat; the wontons will overcook and fall apart.

SIDE PEA SHOOT SALAD

Light and delicate, pea shoots make a refreshing salad and can be paired with a variety of vegetables or fruit, such as cucumber, daikon, mango, or strawberry. I've chosen radishes for this salad, but feel free to experiment.

SERVES 6

6 ounces fresh pea shoots, about 5 to 6 cups, rinsed in a salad spinner

3 radishes, cut into matchsticks

DRESSING:

1 tablespoon fresh lime juice

1 tablespoon fresh orange juice

1 tablespoon soy sauce

2 tablespoons canola oil

1/2 teaspoon finely grated fresh ginger

1 Combine the pea shoots and radish matchsticks in a serving bowl.

2 In a small bowl, whisk together the lime juice, orange juice, soy sauce, oil, and grated ginger. Just before serving the salad, add enough dressing to coat the greens and toss gently. Serve immediately.

BEAN
NOODLE
WHOLE GRAIN

SOUP RUSTIC ROOT VEGETABLE SOUP WITH WILD RICE AND BARLEY

Toothsome root veggies coupled with wild rice and barley make for a pleasant chewiness in this soup. Though the ingredient list is long, it's an easy, uncomplicated soup to make. This recipe makes a large batch and can be frozen.

SERVES 8

1/2 ounce dried porcini mushrooms

2 cups hot water

1 onion, diced

2 tablespoons extra-virgin olive oil

1 whole leek, trimmed, cut in half lengthwise, rinsed, and sliced

1 small to medium rutabaga or 2 parsnips, peeled (or pared with a knife) and diced small

2 cloves garlic, minced

2 tablespoons tomato paste

8 cups chicken stock

4 carrots, peeled and diced small

1 celery root or 2 stalks celery, peeled and diced small

1/3 cup barley*

1/3 cup wild rice (not the quick-cooking variety)

1 teaspoon kosher salt, plus more to taste

2 teaspoons chopped fresh thyme leaves or 1/2 teaspoon dried thyme

3 to 4 tablespoons minced fresh parsley

Freshly ground black pepper

1 In a small bowl, soak the porcini mushrooms in hot water for 10 to 15 minutes. Drain, but save the soaking water to add to the soup. Chop the mushrooms finely.

2 In a soup pot over medium heat, sauté the onion in the olive oil until soft, about 6 minutes. Add the leek and rutabaga and cook until leek is soft, another 6 to 8 minutes, stirring often. Add garlic and sauté another 1 or 2 minutes. Mix in tomato paste.

3 Add the chopped porcini and the soaking water (being careful to leave any grit in the bottom of the bowl), chicken stock, carrots, celery root (or celery), barley, wild rice, 1 teaspoon salt, and thyme and bring to a boil. Reduce to a simmer, cover partially, and cook until the barley and wild rice are tender but not mushy, 50 to 55 minutes. Stir in the parsley, and add additional salt and some pepper to taste.

* This soup is also delicious substituting 2/3 cup farro for the wild rice and barley.

PAIR WITH SIDE ON PAGE 126.

SIDE FOUGASSE

Of all the breads Martha's Vineyard architect and bread baker extraordinaire Kate Warner makes for friends, this is the most popular. It is a chewy, crunchy bread with olive oil, cheese, salt, and pepper on top. Fougasse is a French version of focaccia, both words meaning hearth or flame. This is a weekend bread because it takes time to rise, but the recipe is not hard to follow: Kate gives detailed instructions for the novice baker.

SERVES 8

1 3/8 cups lukewarm water

3/4 teaspoon instant yeast (you can use active dry yeast, but instant is preferable)

3 1/4 cups white bread flour, plus more for dusting

1 1/2 teaspoons kosher salt, plus more for topping

Extra-virgin olive oil

Freshly ground black pepper

Parmigiano-Reggiano cheese, grated

6 to 8 pieces ice

1 Put the water in the bowl of a standing mixer; add the yeast, then add the flour and salt. Using the dough hook, mix for 5 minutes on the second speed. Scrape the sides of the bowl down to incorporate all the flour. You want the dough to be moderately developed and somewhat sticky: neither slack nor stiff. Add a bit more water if the dough is too stiff. If you can pull the dough without it breaking it's ready. You can also do the mixing and kneading by hand. The goal is to mix it together and then knead without adding any additional flour. A scraper is an essential tool in making this method work.

2 If kneading by hand, scrape the dough into a bowl. In either case, cover the dough with plastic wrap. Let it rise for 1 hour at room temperature (70° to 75°). If your kitchen is too cool, put a heating pad on the lower oven rack, turn the pad to low, and put the bowl of dough on the upper rack.

3 Scrape the dough out onto a lightly floured surface. Lightly sprinkle the top of the dough with flour and then fold the left side into the middle, the right side into the middle, and then the same for the top and bottom. Pick the dough up with a scraper and put back in the bowl, seam side down, to rise for 1 hour.

4 Gently scrape the dough out of the bowl onto a lightly floured surface, being careful not to deflate it. Lightly flour the top and pull it out into a loose rectangle. Fold it in half lengthwise to form a log and then divide it in half. Very gently shape the halves into balls; cover with a dishtowel and let rest for 10 minutes.

5 Pull each ball out a bit to form an oval. Lay the ovals on a lightly floured surface or lightly floured dishtowel, dust with flour, and cover with a dishtowel. Let the dough rise at room temperature (70° to 75°) for about 45 minutes, more or less depending on the temperature of the room. When you poke the dough, it should stay indented and slowly rise back a little but still show where the indentation was.

6 In the meantime, place a baking stone in the lower third of the oven with a cast iron pan beneath it and preheat to 450° for 45 minutes prior to baking.

7 Liberally sprinkle a pizza peel or a rimless or upside-down cookie sheet with flour or cornmeal. Place 1 oval on the peel or sheet and pull into a long triangular shape. Brush lightly with olive oil, sprinkle with a small amount of salt and pepper on top and a good amount of Parmesan. Using a pizza cutter or sharp knife, make cuts in the middle of the dough to form slits—don't cut all the way to the edge. Pull the dough apart a little so it resembles a leaf or flame.

8 Quickly transfer the dough to the stone, throw 6 to 8 pieces of ice in the cast iron pan, and quickly close the door so as to not lose the steam you have just created.

9 Bake until golden brown and crusty, about 15 minutes. Let the bread cool a little on a cooling rack and serve immediately. Repeat with the second oval of dough. If you are not going to eat them fairly soon after they are baked, reheat them a little to recrisp them before serving. If you are not eating them that day, freeze them: Take the bread out at least an hour before serving to thaw, and then reheat.

PAIR WITH SOUP ON PAGE 124.

SOUP WINTER VEGETABLE SOUP WITH BARLEY

Chock full of vegetables and barley, this soup gets a nice flavor from the addition of Parmesan rinds during cooking, plus the fresh herbs at the end. You can cut the rind off a hunk of Parmigiano-Reggiano cheese or check out your cheese department, which sometimes sells the rinds together in a container. If Parmesan rinds are unavailable, you can substitute a quart of chicken broth for the water to help flavor the soup. If you have basil pesto, you can add a dollop of that into each soup bowl instead of chopping the parsley and basil. Freeze any leftovers.

SERVES 10

1 large onion, diced

2 tablespoons extra-virgin olive oil

1 large or 2 small whole leeks (use all but tough green parts), trimmed, cut in half lengthwise, rinsed, and thinly sliced (about 2 cups)

2 cloves garlic, finely minced

4 medium carrots, peeled and diced (about 1 1/2 cups)

2 medium stalks celery, trimmed and diced (about 1 cup)

2 cups thinly shredded Savoy cabbage (optional)

10 cups water, plus more if needed

1/2 cup pearl barley, rinsed

2 medium Parmigiano-Reggiano cheese rinds

2 teaspoons dried oregano

2 to 3 teaspoons kosher salt

1 medium zucchini, trimmed and diced (about 2 cups)

1 cup 1/2-inch pieces green beans

1 (28-ounce) can diced tomatoes, with juices

1/3 cup minced fresh parsley

1/2 cup chopped fresh basil

Grated Parmigiano-Reggiano cheese, to taste

1 In a soup pot over medium heat, sauté the onion in olive oil until golden and soft, 8 to 10 minutes. Add the leeks and garlic and sauté a few minutes more. Add the carrots, celery, cabbage, water, barley, Parmesan rinds, oregano, and salt and bring to a boil. Reduce heat to medium-low and simmer, partially covered, stirring occasionally, for 25 minutes.

2 Add the zucchini, green beans, and tomatoes and juices; bring to a simmer again and continue cooking on medium-low until the barley is tender, about 20 minutes more.

3 Remove the Parmesan rinds and discard. Adjust the seasonings, adding more salt if necessary. Add the fresh herbs. Ladle soup into bowls, and add a spoonful of Parmesan cheese.

SIDE OLIVE OIL AND PARMESAN DIPPING OIL

A simple side of bread and dipping oil go well with this vegetable soup. If you want to go further, a mini cheese platter is another great addition.

SERVES 4 TO 6

1/2 cup good-quality extra-virgin olive oil

1 sprig of rosemary or two sprigs of thyme

2 tablespoons grated Parmigiano-Reggiano cheese

Nice bread, sliced, for dipping

Heat the olive oil and rosemary in a small skillet until the olive oil starts to sizzle. Turn off and let sit for 5 to 10 minutes. Mix in the Parmesan cheese and pour into a small dish for dipping bread.

`SOUP` # RED LENTIL SOUP

Quick and simple to make, this soup cooks in just over a half-hour. The red lentils break down and thicken the soup, flavored by the cumin, cilantro, and fresh lime juice at the end. Lentils, like all beans, offer protein, iron, calcium, thiamin, riboflavin, and niacin. Add the chickpea burgers for a filling lunch or dinner.

SERVES 6

1 onion, diced

2 tablespoons extra-virgin olive oil

1 whole leek, trimmed, cut in half lengthwise, rinsed, and sliced

2 stalks celery, diced

4 medium carrots, peeled and diced

2 cloves garlic, finely minced

1/2 teaspoon curry powder

2 teaspoons ground cumin

1 1/2 cups red lentils, rinsed

7 cups water

Salt

1/3 to 1/2 cup chopped fresh cilantro

2 tablespoons freshly squeezed lime juice (from about 2 limes)

1 In a large stockpot, sauté the onion in the oil over medium heat, stirring occasionally, until golden, about 7 minutes. Add the leek, celery, and carrots and sauté 3 to 4 minutes. Add the garlic, curry, and cumin and cook just briefly to bring out the flavor of the spices, about 30 seconds, stirring constantly. Add the lentils and water and bring to a boil. Turn the heat to low and simmer, covered, 25 to 30 minutes, stirring occasionally and removing any foam that forms at the top early on. Season with salt.

2 Just before serving, add the cilantro and fresh lime juice to taste.

PAIR WITH SIDE ON PAGE 132.

SIDE CHICKPEA BURGERS WITH YOGURT SAUCE

These mini chickpea burgers—a combination of grain and bean—are my version of falafels that are not fried. With a simple, creamy yogurt sauce and pita triangles, they made a great side for lentil soup.

SERVES 4 TO 6

3/4 cup water

1/2 cup fine or medium bulghur wheat (labeled No. 2 in a Middle Eastern store)

1 1/4 teaspoons kosher salt

1 small to medium red onion

1/4 cup minced cilantro or parsley

3/4 cup cooked chickpeas, rinsed well

1 teaspoon ground cumin

1/8 teaspoon cayenne pepper

1/2 to 1 cup panko or other bread crumbs

Olive oil, for sautéing

Yogurt sauce (recipe follows)

Pita bread

YOGURT SAUCE:

1 cup plain yogurt

1/4 teaspoon ground cumin

2 teaspoons extra-virgin olive oil

2 teaspoons freshly squeezed lemon juice

1 clove garlic, finely minced

2 tablespoons chopped cilantro or mint

1 Place water in a small saucepan and bring to a boil. Add the bulghur and 1/2 teaspoon salt, turn burner off, cover, and let the bulghur sit for at least 20 minutes.

2 Place onion and cilantro or parsley in a food processor and finely chop. Add the cooked bulghur, chickpeas, cumin, cayenne, and the remaining 3/4 teaspoon salt and pulse until chickpeas are chopped but not pureed.

3 Turn into a bowl and mix in 1/2 cup bread crumbs. The mixture will be a bit moist; if it seems too moist, mix in additional bread crumbs. Form into 8 small patties about 2 1/2 inches wide by 1/2 inch high.

4 To cook the patties, pour a film of oil into a skillet over medium heat and sauté until patties are golden and hot, about 5 minutes on each side.

5 In a bowl, combine the yogurt, cumin, olive oil, lemon juice, garlic, and cilantro or mint. Mix well. Serve the burgers with yogurt sauce spooned over the top and pita bread on the side.

PAIR WITH SOUP ON PAGE 131.

`SOUP` # VEGETARIAN ASIAN NOODLE SOUP

I love the flavors in this soup, plus the variety of vegetables. But what makes it irresistible for me are the noodles. Some of the testers favored fresh Chinese noodles or dried thin noodles over the udon—you'll want to experiment to find your own favorites. Whatever type you use, the key is to not overcook them.

SERVES 4 TO 6

6 to 8 ounces Asian noodles, such as fresh Chinese noodles, dried thin noodles, udon, or ramen

2 cups sliced shiitake mushrooms

1 whole leek, trimmed, cut in half lengthwise, rinsed, and sliced

1 tablespoon canola oil

1 tablespoon grated fresh ginger

1 clove garlic, minced

1 stalk lemongrass, trimmed of tough leaves, inner center minced

6 cups water

1/2 pound extra-firm tofu, diced medium

1 carrot, peeled and cut into matchsticks

2 small heads baby bok choy, thinly sliced

3 tablespoons soy sauce

1 tablespoon rice vinegar

1/2 teaspoon chili paste or hot sauce

3 scallions, green parts only, thinly sliced

1/3 cup chopped fresh cilantro (optional)

1 Cook the noodles in a large pot of salted water according to package directions, minus 1 to 2 minutes for al dente. Drain, then run under cold water to stop the cooking. Set aside.

2 In a soup pot over medium heat, sauté the mushrooms and leek in the oil until mushrooms begin to cook and leek softens. Add the ginger, garlic, and lemongrass and continue cooking and stirring for 1 to 2 minutes.

3 Add the water and tofu and bring to a boil, then simmer for 5 minutes. Add the carrot and bok choy, cook another 2 minutes; remove from heat. Season with soy sauce, rice vinegar, and hot sauce. When ready to serve, divide the desired amount of noodles and scallions among the bowls and ladle the hot soup over them. Add cilantro to garnish, if using.

PAIR WITH SIDE ON PAGE 134.

SIDE SCALLION PANCAKES

These are best cooked just before eating. Serve with a dipping sauce—either a ponzu-type sauce or one you make yourself with soy sauce and a bit of fresh ginger.

SERVES 6 AS A SIDE

2 tablespoons canola oil

1 1/2 cups thinly sliced scallions, white and green parts

2 teaspoons plus a pinch kosher salt

2 cups all-purpose flour

2 eggs, lightly beaten

1 1/2 to 1 3/4 cups water

1/4 teaspoon red pepper flakes

2 tablespoons minced fresh chives or basil (optional)

1 Heat 1 tablespoon oil in a medium skillet over medium heat and sauté the scallions for 1 to 2 minutes, stirring constantly. Season with a pinch of salt. Place in a medium bowl; wipe out the skillet with a paper towel.

2 Add flour, eggs, and 1 1/2 cups water to the scallions and mix with a fork. Season with red pepper flakes, chives or basil (if using), and 2 teaspoons salt. The batter should be similar to a pancake batter; add a bit more water to thin, if needed.

3 Heat about 2 teaspoons oil in the skillet over medium-high heat. Add about one-third of the batter to nearly fill the pan, tilting or spreading the batter into a thin pancake. Cook until golden on both sides, flipping halfway through, about 3 to 5 minutes total. Cool pancake on a paper towel. Fold and cut into triangles. Repeat with the remaining batter. Serve hot with dipping sauce and the soup.

PAIR WITH SOUP ON PAGE 133.

SOUP KALE AND VEGETABLE SOUP WITH FARRO

This is similar to an Italian vegetable soup, only better (and easier), with added nutrients from the kale and a quick-cooking and delicious Italian grain called farro. A type of wheat imported from Italy, farro offers a mildly chewy, nutty flavor, similar to barley (which can be substituted if farro is unavailable). For a vegetarian version, add water instead of stock plus two Parmigiano-Reggiano cheese rinds.

SERVES 6

2 tablespoons extra-virgin olive oil

1 onion, diced

1 whole leek, trimmed, cut in half lengthwise, rinsed, and sliced

2 cloves garlic, minced

8 cups chicken stock

2 large carrots (about 2 cups), cut in half lengthwise and sliced

2 stalks celery, diced

1 tablespoon chopped fresh thyme

1/2 cup farro*

1 to 2 teaspoons kosher salt

1/2 bunch (about 3 cups lightly packed) kale, stems removed, chopped

1 (14-ounce) can diced tomatoes, with juices

Freshly ground black pepper

Parmigiano-Reggiano cheese, to taste

1 In a soup pot, heat the oil and sauté the onion over medium heat for 8 minutes, stirring occasionally. Add the leek and sauté until softened, about 4 minutes. Add garlic and sauté another 1 to 2 minutes. Add stock, carrots, celery, thyme, farro, and 1 teaspoon salt and bring to a boil. Turn heat to low and simmer, partially covered, for 15 minutes.

2 Stir in chopped kale and the tomatoes. Bring to a boil again, turn to low, and simmer, partially covered, 15 to 20 minutes, until farro and kale are tender. Taste the soup and add additional salt if needed, plus a few grinds of pepper. Top each bowl with Parmesan cheese for more depth of flavor.

* Using barley instead of farro: Farro can be found in Whole Foods Market in the dried pasta section, or in an Italian market. If you can't find farro, use 1/3 cup of barley and increase the cooking time in step one to 30 minutes, for a total of about 50 minutes.

PAIR WITH SIDE ON PAGE 138.

SIDE FRESH MOZZARELLA AND ROASTED RED PEPPER SANDWICHES

SERVES 4

8 slices French or sourdough bread

2 tablespoons extra-virgin olive oil or butter, at room temperature

3/4 pound whole fresh mozzarella, sliced in 1/4-inch-thick rounds

2 red bell peppers, roasted and sliced (see page 34)

Salt

1 cup fresh arugula or basil leaves

1 Brush 1 side of each bread slice with olive oil or slather with butter. Place 4 pieces of bread on a work surface oiled side down. Top each with a layer of mozzarella, a layer of roasted pepper, a pinch of salt, and a few leaves of arugula or basil. Place the other pieces of bread on top, oiled side up.

2 Heat a large skillet, over medium heat, or use a panini press and cook the sandwiches until cheese is softened and bread is lightly toasted on both sides, about 4 minutes.

PAIR WITH SOUP ON PAGE 137.

SOUP **QUICK FRENCH LENTIL SOUP**

This lentil soup uses the French green lentils, also called lentils de Puy. These are smaller than brown lentils, cook quicker, and hold their shape for a better appearance. You can experiment by adding different fresh herbs, such as thyme or oregano, or other greens instead of parsley, such as spinach.

SERVES 4 TO 6

1 onion, diced small
2 tablespoons extra-virgin olive oil
1 whole leek, trimmed, cut in half
     lengthwise, rinsed, and sliced
2 cloves garlic, minced
1/2 cup red or white wine (optional)
2 carrots, peeled and diced
2 stalks celery, diced
1/4 cup minced fresh parsley
6 cups water
2 bay leaves
1 1/4 cups French green lentils, picked
     through and rinsed
1 (14-ounce) can diced tomatoes, with
     juices
2 teaspoons umeboshi vinegar* or
     freshly squeezed lemon juice
1 teaspoon kosher salt
Freshly ground black pepper

1 In a heavy-bottomed soup pot, sauté the onion in the oil over medium heat for 8 to 10 minutes. Add the leek and garlic and cook another 2 to 3 minutes, stirring often. Add the wine and cook for 1 minute.

2 Add carrots, celery, half the parsley, the water, bay leaves, and lentils. Bring to a boil, then simmer, partially covered, for 10 minutes. Add the tomatoes and continue simmering, 20 to 25 minutes, or until lentils are tender.

3 Remove the bay leaf and add umeboshi vinegar or lemon juice, salt, and pepper. Adjust seasonings and simmer for an additional few minutes. Add remaining parsley just before serving.

* Found in natural food markets, umeboshi vinegar is made from the brine of pickled plums. It is both tangy and salty, and livens up bean soups.

PAIR WITH SIDE ON PAGE 140.

SIDE # HONEY-DIJON SALMON BITES

Cutting the salmon into bite-size squares and baking them in a soy, honey, and lemon sauce cuts the cooking time to just 12 minutes and creates a fun presentation. To make the pieces look as uniform as possible, get a piece of salmon that's not too thick or thin—about 1 inch thick. Ask your fishmonger to skin the fish for you.

SERVES 4

1 pound fresh salmon, skin removed
1 1/2 teaspoons honey
1 tablespoon freshly squeezed lemon
  juice
1 teaspoon Dijon mustard
1 tablespoon soy sauce
1 clove garlic, minced
2 tablespoons extra-virgin olive oil
1 1/2 tablespoons minced fresh parsley
  or chives

1 Preheat the oven to 375°. Cut the salmon into bite-size squares, about 1 inch across. Try to cut them as uniformly as possible to create an appealing presentation. Place in an 8-inch square Pyrex dish or glass pie plate.

2 In a small bowl, whisk together the honey, lemon juice, Dijon, soy sauce, garlic, olive oil, and 1 tablespoon parsley or chives. Pour over the salmon, coating all sides. Bake for 10 to 12 minutes, until just done.

3 Carefully lift the pieces with a spatula to a nice platter or plate and place a toothpick in the middle of each piece. Sprinkle with the remaining parsley or chives and serve.

PAIR WITH SOUP ON PAGE 139.

SOUP PORTUGUESE WHITE BEAN AND GREENS STEW

Rich with fennel and oregano broth, sun-dried tomatoes, carrots, potatoes, and hearty braised greens, you'll never miss the usual sausage that makes this a Portuguese favorite. This recipe, created by Cathi DiCocco was first served at Café DiCocoa, located in Bethel, Maine, on a night featuring the food of Portugal.

SERVES 8 TO 10

BEANS:

1 pound dried white beans or 5 (15-ounce) cans, rinsed and drained*

1 whole garlic bulb

3 bay leaves

2 teaspoons dried oregano

2 teaspoons salt, plus more to taste

2 teaspoons whole fennel seeds that have been lightly crushed in a spice grinder or mortar and pestle

STEW:

1 large Spanish onion, diced large

6 cloves garlic, finely chopped

1 pinch red pepper flakes

2 tablespoons extra-virgin olive oil

1 large bunch of greens, such as kale, collards, or Swiss chard, washed, stemmed, and coarsely chopped

8 medium carrots, cut into chunks

4 medium potatoes, peeled and cut into chunks

1/2 cup sun-dried tomatoes packed in olive oil, julienned

2 cups chopped fresh tomatoes, or 1 (15-ounce) can diced tomatoes, with juices

Freshly ground black pepper

1 to 2 tablespoons imported aged sherry vinegar

1 If using canned beans, set them aside in a large pot with enough water to cover, about 10 cups, and begin with step 3. To cook dried beans, first pick through them to remove any shriveled or broken ones. Rinse thoroughly and drain. Place rinsed beans in a large stockpot and add cool water to cover by 4 inches. Peel off and discard the outer papery part of the garlic bulb and cut bulb in half crosswise; add to pot. Add the bay leaves, 1 teaspoon oregano, 1 teaspoon salt, and 1 teaspoon fennel seeds. Cover and bring to a rolling boil. Give it a stir, cover, and lower the heat; simmer 15 minutes. Turn off heat and let soak, covered, for 1 hour.

2 Drain the liquid from the beans; remove and reserve the bay leaves and garlic. Put the beans in the same pot and cover with 1 inch fresh water (about 10 cups). Add the reserved bay leaves. Squeeze the softened garlic from the halved garlic bulb and add to beans. Add the remaining oregano, salt, and fennel. Bring to a boil; partially cover and simmer until beans are soft, about 1 1/2 hours, adding water as needed to keep beans submerged. Set aside.

3 To make the stew, in large skillet over medium heat, sauté the onion, garlic, and red pepper flakes in olive oil for 5 to 6 minutes. Add the greens and braise until tender, about 10 minutes. Add water as necessary to keep the greens from sticking to the pan.

4 Add carrots, potatoes, sun-dried tomatoes, and fresh or canned tomatoes with juice. Stir and simmer until all veggies are nearly done, about 15 minutes.

continued

5 Add the veggies to the pot with the beans. Give it a good stir and simmer over low heat until the flavors marry and the potatoes and carrots are tender, about 5 minutes. Taste for salt and pepper. Remove from heat and stir in the sherry vinegar.

* The restaurant uses dried, organic cannellini beans; navy beans can also be used. If you are using canned beans, you will want to add the seasonings, (1 teaspoon oregano, 2 teaspoons fennel seed, 3 bay leaves), to the veggie sauté as it cooks. Add the finished sauté to the large pot that holds the beans and water.

NOTES FROM THE KITCHEN:

—If you like a thicker stew, feel free to blend 2 cups of cooked beans with some of its broth. Add it back to the pot and stir.

—Dried beans work better than canned in this recipe because they have a chance to drink up the oregano and fennel-scented broth while they rehydrate.

—To brighten up the stew before serving you can stir in some fresh chopped parsley or oregano. A lemon wedge is nice served alongside the bowl for an additional kick.

—This stew gets better as it sits. Keep refrigerated for up to 4 days. Add a small amount of water to thin before reheating or freeze in individual size portions for a delicious meal later on.

—Thick chilled bean stew is wonderful blended into a "hummus dip" and served with raw veggie crudités or pita crisps.

`SIDE` PORTUGUESE TAPAS

Also on the menu for the night of Portuguese foods at Café DiCocoa were these tapas dishes. I recommend some combination of the following dishes, arranged artistically on a platter and served alongside the white bean "sopa." Many of these tapas can be bought and added to the platter.

Goat cheese and pine nut crostini

Hot olives

Marinated fire-roasted artichokes

Manchego (Spanish sheep's milk cheese)

Quince paste

Fig bread

Marcona almonds

Hard-boiled eggs dusted with smoked paprika

Red grapes

SOUP **LENTIL AND VEGETABLE SOUP**

The small, mottled green French lentils cook very quickly and keep their defined shape, perfect for this simple but satisfying soup. Cook the lentils separately to keep them from dominating the soup.

SERVES 4 TO 6

2/3 cup petite French lentils (de Puy), rinsed

1 bay leaf

1 onion, diced

2 tablespoons extra-virgin olive oil

1 whole leek, trimmed, cut in half lengthwise, rinsed, and sliced

2 to 3 cloves garlic, finely minced

3 carrots, peeled and diced

2 stalks celery, diced

7 cups water

2 teaspoons dried oregano

1 (14-ounce) can diced tomato, with juices

1 to 2 teaspoons kosher salt

1 large bunch spinach, stems cut off and chopped, or 4 to 5 cups baby spinach, loosely chopped

Freshly ground black pepper

1 Fill a saucepan with about 2 quarts water and bring to a boil. Add the lentils and bay leaf and simmer, partially covered, 20 to 25 minutes. Check a few lentils for doneness; they shouldn't be hard, but not mushy either. Drain, and shake the strainer a few times to let the steam escape and keep the lentils from deflating. Set aside.

2 While the lentils are cooking, in a soup pot, sauté the onion in the oil over medium heat until soft and translucent, 6 to 8 minutes, stirring occasionally. Add the leek, garlic, carrots, and celery; sauté another 4 to 5 minutes, stirring. Add the water, oregano, tomato, and 1 teaspoon salt and bring to a boil. Reduce heat to low, partially cover, and simmer until the vegetables are cooked, about 25 minutes.

3 Stir in the spinach and lentils and simmer on low for 2 to 3 minutes until spinach is wilted. Taste the soup and add additional salt and pepper to taste.

SIDE PITA PIZZAS WITH FRESH MOZZARELLA, TOMATO, AND BASIL

Pita bread makes a surprisingly workable base for fresh homemade pizzas that you can put together quickly. Make these individual pita pizzas with the smaller-sized pitas or the somewhat larger six-inch pitas, adjusting amounts to the number of people being served. The fresher and softer the pita bread, the better. In the winter, I use fresh cherry tomatoes because they usually still taste like tomatoes; otherwise, use fresh garden tomatoes.

SERVES 6

2 cups fresh cherry tomatoes or 2 whole tomatoes
10 to 12 fresh basil leaves
2 tablespoons extra-virgin olive oil
Salt
1 clove garlic, finely minced
6 (6-inch) pita breads
8 small fresh mozzarella balls, sliced about 1/4 inch thick

1 Preheat the oven to 350°. Cut the tops off the cherry or regular tomatoes and gently squeeze over the sink to remove some of the seeds. Chop the tomatoes into small, dice-size pieces. Chop 6 basil leaves. Put tomatoes and basil in a small bowl with 1 tablespoon olive oil, a few pinches of salt, and the minced garlic.

2 Lay out the pita breads on a baking tray (keeping them whole, not split apart). Brush the tops with the remaining 1 tablespoon olive oil. Top with pieces of mozzarella, partially covering the pita yet leaving some gaps. Top the mozzarella with tomatoes and bake in the oven until the cheese melts, 8 to 10 minutes. (Don't let the cheese burn or the pita get too crispy.)

3 Meanwhile, tear or sliver the remaining basil leaves. Remove pitas from the oven and top with the remaining fresh basil leaves before serving. Slice with a pizza cutter.

CHILIS
GUMBOS
CHOWDERS

SOUP **BLACK BEAN AND BUTTERNUT SQUASH CHILI WITH CILANTRO PESTO**

Katie Le Lievre, owner of HipShake Caterers in Boston, makes a vegetarian chili that combines black beans, corn, and butternut squash that already has a cult following in my neck of the woods. (It also tastes good with shredded chicken.)

SERVES 6 TO 8

2 large onions, coarsely chopped

2 tablespoons extra-virgin olive oil

4 cloves garlic, minced

2 bay leaves

1 tablespoon ground cumin

1 tablespoon dried oregano

1/2 teaspoon freshly ground black pepper

1 tablespoon chili powder

1/4 teaspoon ground cloves

1/8 teaspoon cayenne pepper

2 (28-ounce) cans whole tomatoes, with juices

4 cups 1/2-inch-diced butternut squash (from about 1 medium squash)

2 to 3 cups water

2 cups cooked black beans

Kernels from 3 to 4 ears fresh corn (about 2 cups)

2 to 3 teaspoons kosher salt

Cilantro pesto (recipe follows) or chopped cilantro

CILANTRO PESTO:

1/3 cup walnut pieces, toasted

1 bunch cilantro, washed and tough stems removed (about 1 cup)

2 cloves garlic, minced

1/2 cup canola or olive oil, or a mix

Salt

1 In a large soup pot over medium heat, sauté the onions in oil until translucent, 10 to 15 minutes. Add garlic and sauté another 2 minutes. Add spices and continue cooking, stirring to prevent burning, about 1 minute. Add tomatoes and break apart with a masher. Add squash and 2 cups of the water. Bring to a boil, turn down heat to a simmer, and cover. Let simmer until squash is tender, about 20 minutes.

2 Add the black beans, corn, and the additional water if needed, and simmer to let flavors blend, 5 minutes. Remove bay leaves. Season with salt.

3 To make the pesto, purée the walnuts, cilantro, garlic, and oil in a food processor until smooth. Add salt to taste. Serve the soup with cilantro pesto on top or with plain chopped cilantro, if you prefer.

PAIR WITH SIDE ON PAGE 152.

SIDE CORNBREAD

SERVES 6 TO 8

Vegetable oil, for pan
1 1/2 cups all-purpose flour
1 1/2 cups cornmeal
1/2 cup sugar
2 teaspoons baking powder
1 teaspoon baking soda
1 teaspoon salt
2 eggs
1 1/2 cups buttermilk
6 tablespoons unsalted butter

1 Preheat the oven to 350°. Lightly oil a medium cast-iron skillet or an 8-inch square baking dish.

2 Whisk the flour, cornmeal, sugar, baking powder, baking soda, and salt together in a large bowl.

3 Mix the eggs and buttermilk together in another bowl. Melt the butter, let cool slightly, and add to the liquid ingredients.

4 Add the wet ingredients to the dry and mix with a wooden spoon. Pour into the skillet or baking dish and bake for about 25 minutes, or until a toothpick comes out clean.

PAIR WITH SOUP ON PAGE 151.

SOUP BLACK BEAN AND TURKEY CHILI

For a little more depth of flavor, there's a bit of chocolate and molasses in this chili, but feel free to try it without, especially if you like the tomato flavor to be more prominent. You can always add a bit of shredded cheese or sliced avocado on top as an additional garnish.

SERVES 6 TO 8

2 tablespoons plus 2 teaspoons extra-virgin olive oil

1 large onion, diced

1 red bell pepper, diced

1 small green bell pepper, diced

2 cloves garlic, minced

2 tablespoons chili powder

1 teaspoon ground cumin

1 (28-ounce) can crushed or diced tomatoes, with juices

3 to 4 cups water

2 teaspoons dried oregano

1 dried chipotle pepper or 1/8 teaspoon cayenne or ground chipotle pepper*

1 pound ground white- or dark-meat turkey

1 (15-ounce) can black beans

Kernels from 2 ears fresh corn (about 1 cup)

1 tablespoon unsweetened cocoa or 1 ounce (1 square) dark chocolate (optional)

1 tablespoon molasses (optional)

Salt and freshly ground black pepper

1/3 cup chopped cilantro, for garnish

1 In a large heavy pot over medium heat, place 2 tablespoons olive oil and the onion and sauté, about 5 minutes. Add the bell peppers and continue to cook another 3 to 4 minutes. Add the garlic, chili powder, and cumin and stir for another minute.

2 Add the tomatoes, water, oregano, and chipotle pepper and bring to a boil. Reduce heat to medium-low and simmer, covered, about 10 minutes.

3 While the chili is simmering, cook the turkey in 2 teaspoons oil in a nonstick skillet over medium heat, breaking it up as you go, just until it loses its pink color. Drain the fat and add the turkey to the chili, along with the beans, corn, cocoa, molasses, and salt and pepper to taste. Bring to a boil again, and then simmer another 10 to 15 minutes until all the flavors are incorporated. Taste again for seasoning and add additional salt and pepper if needed. Remove the chipotle pepper.

4 Ladle into bowls and top with the chopped cilantro.

* Dried chipotle peppers are found in grocery stores with other dried chiles. Essentially a smoked jalapeno pepper, dried chipotles add flavor to chilis. Drop one into the pot while the chili is cooking and remove at the end as you would with a bay leaf.

PAIR WITH SIDE ON PAGE 154.

SIDE MAC AND CHEESE MINIS

Making mac 'n cheese in ramekins provides a handy sidekick for a soup, one that kids love.

SERVES 6

1/2 pound cavatappi, fusilli, or rotini
Salt and freshly ground black pepper
1 tablespoon extra-virgin olive oil
3 tablespoons butter
1 shallot, finely minced
3 tablespoons all-purpose flour
1 teaspoon Dijon mustard
1 1/2 cups milk
2 cups shredded cheddar cheese
1 1/2 cups shredded Monterey Jack
cheese

1 Preheat the oven to 350°. Cook the noodles in boiling, salted water according to package directions minus 1 to 2 minutes for al dente. Drain, shaking the strainer a few times to release all the steam. Pour into a bowl and mix in the olive oil to keep the pasta from sticking.

2 In a saucepan, melt the butter over low heat and add the shallot. Sauté until golden. Whisk in the flour and mustard and cook for a minute or so. Whisk in the milk and heat over medium heat until slightly thickened. Turn the heat off and add the cheese. Stir until melted. Add salt and pepper to taste.

3 Pour the sauce over the pasta, stir well, and fill the ramekins. Bake until golden brown and hot, about 20 minutes.

PAIR WITH SOUP ON PAGE 153.

SOUP **CHRIS OSBORN'S KAHLUA CHILI**

I'm lucky to get another great recipe from Christopher Osborn, the chef/owner of Better Life Food, a catering services and culinary products company located in Newton Upper Falls, Massachusetts, and former owner of the Depot Coffee Shoppe, also in Newton. This time, he shares his recipe for Kahlua chili, a slightly sweet and slightly spicy combination of beef, beans, and tomatoes. You can substitute strong coffee for the Kahlua, a coffee liqueur, or mix it with half Kahlua and half coffee, which is delicious. For a little something extra, top with cheddar cheese, a dollop of sour cream, and some chopped scallions. This is a great one-bowl meal when served with honey cornbread muffins.

SERVES 6

1 medium onion, diced
1 tablespoons corn oil or olive oil
2 cloves minced garlic
1 1/2 pounds 80-percent-lean ground beef
1 medium green bell pepper, diced
1 (14-ounce) can diced tomato, with juices
1 (28-ounce) can crushed tomatoes, with juices
2 (15-ounce) cans kidney beans, drained and rinsed
1 teaspoon dried oregano
3/4 teaspoon dried marjoram
Heaping 1/4 teaspoon cayenne
3/4 teaspoon ground cumin
1 1/2 tablespoons chili powder
2 tablespoons chopped fresh parsley
2 tablespoons Kahlua
2 tablespoons strong brewed coffee
3 tablespoons dark brown sugar

1 In a medium pot over medium heat, sauté the onion in the oil until translucent, 5 to 6 minutes. Add the garlic and sauté 1 to 2 minutes, stirring often. Add the beef and peppers and cook over medium heat, breaking meat apart, until meat is fully cooked. Skim off fat and reduce to a simmer, 15 to 20 minutes.

2 Meanwhile, in a separate large pot, heat tomatoes and beans over medium heat, 5 minutes. Add spices and parsley, Kahlua, coffee, and sugar and cook 1 hour, stirring frequently. Add beef mixture and continue to heat over medium heat, 3 to 4 minutes. You may need to add some water if the chili is too thick, especially if it needs to be reheated.

SIDE HONEY CORNBREAD MUFFINS

MAKES 12 MUFFINS

3/4 cup canola oil, plus more for muffin
    tin
1/2 cup sugar
8 tablespoons honey
3 eggs
4 teaspoons baking powder
1/2 teaspoon baking soda
1 teaspoon salt
1 1/4 cups cornmeal
2 1/2 cups all-purpose flour
1 cup milk
2 tablespoons butter

1 Preheat the oven to 350°. Grease a 12-cup muffin tin with oil. Combine 3/4 cup oil, the sugar, 6 tablespoons honey, and the eggs in a large bowl. Mix until smooth.

2 Combine the baking powder, baking soda, salt, cornmeal, and flour in another bowl.

3 Add the dry ingredients and the milk to the oil-sugar mixture, alternating dry and wet until combined. Mix until smooth.

4 Spoon batter into the prepared muffin tin, filling the cups three-quarters full. Bake until golden brown, about 20 to 25 minutes.

5 Meanwhile, melt the butter in a small skillet over low heat, or in a microwave-safe bowl in the microwave. Stir in 2 tablespoons honey. Brush the tops of the muffins with the glaze while the muffins are still warm.

SOUP **SHRIMP AND CORN CHOWDER**

Shrimp, corn, potatoes, and fresh herbs make a wonderful combination any time of the year, but especially in the summer when corn is in season.

SERVES 6 TO 8

4 ears fresh corn

2 tablespoons butter

1 onion, diced

1 whole leek, trimmed, cut in half lengthwise, rinsed, and sliced

1 red bell pepper, diced small

1 stalk celery, diced small

2 cups clam broth*

3 cups water

2 medium to large red potatoes, peeled and cut into 1/2-inch dice (about 2 cups)

2 teaspoons chopped fresh thyme leaves

1 pound peeled and deveined small to medium shrimp, cut into halves or thirds

1 cup heavy cream

Salt and freshly ground black pepper

2 tablespoons chopped fresh chives or parsley

1 Hold the corn cobs upright inside a large bowl. Using a chef's knife, slice the kernels off the cob so the kernels fall into the bowl. Reverse your knife and with the dull edge, run down the length of the cob and press out the "milk" and small bits of corn. Set aside, do not discard the cobs.

2 In a soup pot over medium heat, melt the butter and sauté the onion until soft, 5 minutes. Add the leek, red pepper, and celery and sauté another 5 minutes. Add the clam broth, water, potatoes, thyme, and 2 of the corn cobs broken in half, and cook until potatoes are almost soft, 15 to 20 minutes. Add the corn and its scrapings and the shrimp and cook about 5 minutes longer.

3 When the shrimp is cooked, discard the cobs and stir in the cream. Add salt and pepper to taste and garnish with fresh chives or parsley.

* Check with your fishmonger to see if they make their own clam broth. If they do, this will give the soup a nice, fresh flavor.

PAIR WITH SIDE ON PAGE 160.

SIDE ROASTED EGGPLANT WITH TOMATO SALAD

Rosemary Gambino is the owner of Rosecuts Salon on Martha's Vineyard. An experienced cook, this dish is one of her summer favorites: roasted eggplants that sit and marinate with a fresh tomato salad on top. Use flavorful summer garden tomatoes; colorful heirloom tomatoes would make a great presentation. The recipe works nicely with tender, small eggplants (not the long, thin ones).

SERVES 4

2 small eggplants, 6 to 8 inches long
5 tablespoons extra-virgin olive oil
Salt and freshly ground black pepper
4 cups large-diced fresh tomatoes
1 tablespoon chopped fresh oregano
   leaves
1 tablespoon chopped fresh parsley
1 clove garlic, finely minced
2 tablespoons red wine vinegar
6 basil leaves

1 Preheat the oven to 350°. Line a baking sheet with parchment paper. Cut the eggplants in half lengthwise, brush the flesh with 1 tablespoon of the olive oil, and season with salt and pepper. Place on the prepared baking sheet, cut side down. Bake until eggplant is cooked but not collapsed, 25 to 30 minutes (longer if the eggplants are larger).

2 Meanwhile, place the tomatoes in a bowl with the oregano and parsley.

3 In a small bowl, whisk together the remaining 4 tablespoons olive oil and the garlic, vinegar, and salt to taste. Just before you dress the tomatoes, pour off any tomato juice that might have accumulated in the bowl so it doesn't dilute the dressing. Pour the dressing over the tomatoes.

4 When the eggplant is done, place it cut side up on a nice serving platter. Top with the diced tomato salad and let the two sit and marinate for 2 to 3 hours at room temperature.

5 Tear the basil leaves into pieces and scatter over the tomatoes before serving.

PAIR WITH SOUP ON PAGE 159.

SOUP **BOUILLABAISSE À LA VINEYARD**

This fish-based soup is always popular with Rachel Vaughn's clients. Rachel, a wonderfully creative cook, is a private chef who works in Big Sky, Montana in the winter and Martha's Vineyard in the summer.

SERVES 6

1 cup chopped onion

1 leek, white and light green parts, trimmed, cut in half lengthwise, rinsed, and sliced

1/4 cup extra-virgin olive oil

1 cup finely diced celery

2 cloves garlic, minced

1 large green bell pepper, diced small

1 teaspoon fennel seed, crushed but not totally ground

2 cups dry white wine

1 1/2 cups clam juice

2 cups chicken stock

3 sprigs fresh thyme

1 (28-ounce) can whole Italian tomatoes, with juices, roughly chopped

2 cups peeled, 1/4-inch diced potatoes

2 (2-inch) strips orange peel

2 teaspoons kosher salt

1/4 to 1/2 teaspoon crushed red pepper flakes

1/2 pound shrimp (any size except jumbo), peeled, tails on

2 pounds haddock, cod, or halibut, cut into large pieces

1/2 pound bay or sea scallops

12 littleneck clams or mussels

1 tablespoon chopped fresh basil

1 tablespoon chopped fresh chives

1 tablespoon minced fresh parsley

1 In a large, wide soup pot over medium heat, sauté the onion and leek in the oil for 4 to 6 minutes. Add the celery, garlic, bell peppers, and crushed fennel and continue to cook another 1 to 2 minutes.

2 Add 1 1/2 cups white wine, and bring to a boil. Add the clam juice, chicken stock, thyme, chopped tomatoes, potatoes, orange peel, and salt. Bring to a boil again, then reduce heat and simmer for 10 minutes, until the potatoes are nearly cooked.

3 Add the red pepper flakes and shrimp and lightly simmer, covered, for 2 minutes. Drop in the fish and scallops and cook another 5 minutes. Try to stir the pot only minimally so the fish doesn't break apart.

4 In a separate pot with a lid, bring the remaining 1/2 cup white wine to a boil. Add the clams or mussels, cover, and steam until they open, 5 to 8 minutes. (If your pot is wide enough, you can skip this step and cook the shellfish right in the bouillabaisse, adding the shellfish when you add the shrimp.)

5 Remove the orange peels from the soup, and add the clams or mussels. Sprinkle in the fresh herbs and serve immediately.

PAIR WITH SIDE ON PAGE 163.

SIDE RED PEPPER ROUILLE

SERVES 6

1/2 cup cubed fresh bread or fresh bread crumbs

2 cloves garlic

1 red bell pepper, roasted (see page 34)

4 tablespoons extra-virgin olive oil

1 teaspoon freshly squeezed lemon juice

1/8 teaspoon cayenne pepper

1/2 teaspoon freshly ground black pepper

Salt

1 baguette, sliced on a diagonal

1 Preheat the oven to 350°. Place the bread in a bowl with 3 to 4 tablespoons water to soften. Smash 1 of the garlic cloves with the flat side of a knife. Combine the bell pepper, bread, smashed garlic clove, 2 tablespoons olive oil, lemon juice, cayenne, and black pepper in a blender. Blend until smooth. Add salt to taste.

2 Place the bread slices on a baking sheet and brush the tops with the remaining olive oil. Bake until lightly crisp, 8 to 10 minutes. Cut the remaining garlic clove in half and rub it on the toasted bread.

3 Spoon the red pepper rouille onto the crisp bread and serve one with each bowl of bouillabaisse.

PAIR WITH SOUP ON PAGE 161.

`SOUP` CORN CHOWDER WITH SPICY RED PEPPER

Corn chowder is delicious, but it often needs a boost of flavor. Here, it gets help from a red pepper roasted and pureed with chili powder and cayenne. The smoky flavor of a chipotle powder or smoked paprika makes a nice substitution for the cayenne, which is hot but not smoky. Part of the soup is blended to create additional creaminess.

SERVES 6

1 large red bell pepper
6 ears fresh corn
2 tablespoons butter
1 medium onion, diced
1 whole leek, trimmed, cut in half lengthwise, rinsed, and sliced
1 stalk celery, diced small
2 cloves garlic, finely minced
4 1/2 cups chicken stock
2 cups 1/2-inch-diced potato (about 3/4 pound)
2 teaspoons salt
1 teaspoon chili powder
1/8 teaspoon cayenne pepper, chipotle chili powder, or smoked paprika
1/2 cup heavy cream
2 tablespoons finely minced fresh parsley leaves
Freshly ground black pepper

1 Roast the red pepper (see page 34). Place in a paper bag to steam and set aside.

2 Hold the corn cobs upright inside a large bowl. Using a chef's knife, slice the kernels off the cob, so the kernels fall into the bowl. You should have about 3 cups of corn. Reverse your knife (or use the back of a table knife) and with the dull edge, run down the length of the cob and press out the "milk" and small bits of corn. Set aside.

3 In a soup pot over medium heat, melt the butter and sauté the onion until translucent, about 6 minutes. Add the leek and celery and cook another 5 minutes, stirring occasionally. Add the corn and garlic and sauté 3 to 4 minutes longer, stirring often. Add the stock, potato, and 1 1/2 teaspoons salt. Bring to a boil. Turn to low, cover, and simmer until potatoes are cooked, about 20 minutes.

4 Meanwhile, peel the blackened skin from the red pepper and remove the core. Run it under cold water to remove any black pieces. Place the roasted pepper in a blender with the chili powder and cayenne or smoked chipotle and a pinch of salt. Blend until very smooth, at least 1 minute. Add a tiny bit of water if it won't blend smoothly. Set aside in a small bowl.

5 Purée 1 cup of the corn chowder in a blender and add back to the soup. Add the cream and parsley and test for salt and pepper. Ladle the soup into bowls and with a spoon, swirl about 2 teaspoons of the red pepper puree on the surface of the soup.

SIDE CRAB CAKES

These can be served with a tomato-based cocktail sauce or some of the red pepper puree from the corn chowder with a squeeze of lemon or lime juice added.

SERVES 4 TO 6,
OR MORE AS AN APPETIZER

1 pound fresh or frozen lump blue crabmeat
1/2 cup chopped red onion
1/2 cup diced celery
1 egg, lightly beaten
1/4 cup tiny-diced red bell pepper
2 tablespoons chopped fresh dill
2 tablespoons chopped fresh parsley
1/2 teaspoon hot sauce
1/3 cup mayonnaise
1 tablespoon Dijon mustard
2 tablespoons freshly squeezed lemon juice
3/4 teaspoon kosher salt
Freshly ground black pepper
3/4 to 1 cup panko bread crumbs
Extra-virgin olive oil, for sautéing

1 If using frozen crabmeat, defrost the crab in a strainer. Squeeze out the moisture with your hands.

2 Pulse the red onion and celery in a food processor to mince (not purée). Squeeze the moisture out of the onion-celery mixture with your hands.

3 In a large bowl, combine the onion-celery mixture, egg, red pepper, dill, parsley, hot sauce, mayonnaise, Dijon, lemon juice, salt, and pepper to taste. Gently mix in the crabmeat and bread crumbs. Try not to overmix, adding additional bread crumbs if the mixture is too moist.

4 Shape into crab cakes about 2 inches wide and 1 inch high and refrigerate at least 15 minutes. Just before serving, heat a large skillet over medium-high heat. Coat with olive oil and cook the crab cakes until crisp, 2 to 3 minutes per side.

`SOUP` JIM'S QUAHOG CHOWDER

This recipe is from Jim Miller, a friend who lives on Martha's Vineyard and digs his own quahogs. He explains the recipe's origin this way: "When I moved here I was stunned at what they serve up as 'chowder': thick, gooey glop loaded with corn starch or some other thickener, presumably because people equate thick with good. The opposite is true; true quahog chowder is a soup, not a custard. Driven to desperation, I came up with this recipe."

SERVES 6

6 tablespoons unsalted butter
1 1/2 cups chopped onions
5 pounds quahogs (about 1 dozen), shucked and chopped
4 cups clam juice*
2 to 3 cups red potatoes, diced
1 to 2 teaspoons freshly ground black pepper
4 cups whole milk

1 Melt 3 tablespoons butter in a soup pot over medium heat. Add the onions and sauté until they are translucent, 6 to 8 minutes. Add the quahogs and cook for two minutes, stirring constantly. Add the clam juice, potatoes, and pepper and bring to a boil. Reduce heat to low and simmer, uncovered, for 30 minutes.

2 Turn off the heat and add milk and remaining 3 tablespoons butter. Stir thoroughly, until butter is melted. Cover and let sit for 15 minutes before serving.

* You may want to purchase 1 pint of clam juice to have on hand in case there is not enough natural clam juice from the quahogs, if you are shucking your own. The clam juice is fairly salty and so no salt is added to the soup. For a less-salty version substitute more milk (water or skim milk) for the clam juice.

SIDE CHERRY TOMATO SALAD

SERVES 6

1 1/2 cups cubed French or Italian
   bread
1 tablespoon extra virgin olive oil
1 garlic clove, finely minced
6 to 8 cups mixed baby greens
1 cucumber, peeled, seeded, and diced
1/4 red onion, thinly sliced
2 cups cherry tomatoes, preferably a
   mix of red, yellow, and orange,
   halved or quartered

RED WINE VINAIGRETTE:
2 tablespoons red wine vinegar
5 tablespoons extra virgin olive oil
1/2 teaspoon dried oregano
1 garlic clove, finely minced
Salt and pepper

1 Preheat the oven to 350˚. Place the bread cubes in a bowl and toss them with olive oil and garlic. Spread the bread cubes on a baking sheet and toast them in the oven for 10 to 12 minutes, or until the bread is slightly crisp and brown on the outside but still soft inside.

2 To make the dressing, in a small bowl, whisk the vinegar, oil, oregano, and garlic together. Season with salt and pepper.

3 Place the greens in a salad bowl. Add enough dressing to coat the salad and toss well. Top with cucumber, sliced onion, and cherry tomatoes. Drizzle some of the dressing over the vegetables. Top with croutons.

SOUP CHICKEN GUMBO

Gumbo is a favorite soup of mine. The word gumbo comes from the African word for okra, which I add for its unique taste and thickening ability. You do have to stir your roux while it's first cooking, but otherwise, this soup is not hard to make. If you like sausage, add slices of cooked andouille or kielbasa for more heat.

SERVES 6 TO 8

1/3 cup canola oil

1/2 cup all-purpose flour

2 cups chopped onions

1 green bell pepper, diced

1 red bell pepper, diced

1 1/2 cups diced celery

2 cloves garlic, finely minced

6 to 7 cups hot chicken stock

1 teaspoon dried thyme or 2 teaspoons chopped fresh thyme leaves

2 bay leaves

1 teaspoon Cajun or Creole seasoning or paprika

1/8 to 1/4 teaspoon cayenne pepper (depending how hot the Cajun spice is)

1 to 2 teaspoons kosher salt

3/4 pound okra, sliced into 1/2-inch rounds (about 2 cups)

Kernels from 2 to 3 ears fresh corn (about 1 1/2 cups)

2 boneless chicken breasts (about 1 1/2 pounds), cut into small cubes

Freshly ground black pepper

1/2 cup minced fresh parsley

1/2 teaspoon hot sauce, or more to taste

1 Make the roux: In a heavy stockpot or Dutch oven, combine the oil and flour and stir to make a paste. Place over medium-high heat and stir constantly until the roux is a dark, rich brown (the color of a penny), 12 to 15 minutes. You must stir constantly or the flour mixture will burn.

2 Add the onions, bell peppers, and celery to the roux and sauté until the onions are transparent, 5 to 7 minutes. Once you add the vegetables the roux stops cooking, but continue to stir occasionally because the mixture will be rather thick. Add garlic and stir 1 to 2 minutes.

3 Gradually add 6 cups of the stock, and stir until smooth. Add the thyme, bay leaves, Cajun spice or paprika, cayenne, 1 teaspoon salt, and the okra. Bring to a boil, then lower the heat and simmer, covered, for about 15 minutes. Stir occasionally. Skim off any oil that rises to the surface while cooking.

4 Add the corn and chicken and simmer gently until chicken just turns white and is cooked, 5 to 7 minutes. If you keep the broth at a simmer rather than a boil, the chicken will remain tender.

5 Taste and adjust the seasonings, adding a bit of black pepper. Add the parsley and hot sauce to taste.

SIDE JASMINE RICE

SERVES 6 TO 8

1 1/2 cups jasmine or basmati rice
3 cups water
1/2 teaspoon kosher salt

Bring the rice, water, and salt to a boil in a saucepan. Lower heat to a simmer, cover, and cook for 12 to 15 minutes. When you lift the lid, all the water should be gone. Remove from the stove and let sit 5 minutes, covered. Fluff rice with a fork before serving. Using an ice cream scooper, place a scoop of rice in the center of a wide, shallow soup bowl. Spoon the gumbo around.

TOMATO

SOUPS
+ SIDES

`SOUP` # SYLVIA'S TOMATO BISQUE

Sylvia Hurst, who, with her husband Phil, owns Truett-Hurst Winery in Healdsburg, California, made this creamy and sophisticated tomato soup for a celebration dinner for Julie Coleman, our good friend.

SERVES 4

4 tablespoons (1/2 stick) butter
1 onion, diced
1 (28-ounce) can crushed tomatoes
6 medium tomatoes, peeled, seeded, and chopped (see page 33)
1/4 cup anisette liqueur
1 tablespoon crushed fennel seed
2 to 3 teaspoons kosher salt
1/4 teaspoon freshly ground black pepper
1 cup half-and-half

1 Melt the butter in a soup pot over medium heat, and sauté the onion, covered, for 10 minutes. Add the canned tomatoes, fresh tomatoes, anisette, fennel, salt, and pepper. Simmer for about 30 minutes.

2 Blend soup in batches and return to the pot, stirring in the half-and-half. Season to taste.

SIDE BLACK PEPPER PARMESAN CHEESE TWISTS

Made from frozen puff pastry, these are easy to throw together after making a soup. Bake just before serving.

SERVES 4 TO 6

1/3 cup grated Parmigiano-Reggiano cheese

1/2 teaspoon freshly ground black pepper

1 tablespoon chopped fresh chives or parsley

1 egg

1 tablespoon water

1/2 pound (half a package) Pepperidge Farm Puff Pastry Sheets, defrosted

All-purpose flour, for dusting

1 Preheat the oven to 400°. Mix the cheese, pepper, and chives or parsley together in a small bowl.

2 In another small bowl, whisk the egg and water together.

3 Unfold the pastry sheet on a lightly floured surface. Roll the dough into a 10-by-14-inch rectangle. Cut in half lengthwise. Brush the surface of both halves with the egg mixture and sprinkle one of the halves with about three-quarters of the cheese mixture.

4 Place the remaining half of dough over the filling, egg-brushed side down. Press the edges to seal, and press the dough gently to make the layers stick together or roll lightly with the rolling pin to seal.

5 Using a pizza cutter, cut the dough crosswise into 28 strips, 1/2 inch wide. Twist the strips 4 or 5 times from the middle outward and place on a baking sheet, pressing down the ends. Brush the twists with the egg mixture, and sprinkle the rest of the Parmesan mixture on top.

6 Bake until golden brown, 12 to 15 minutes. Cool slightly on a wire rack. Serve immediately.

SOUP SUMMER GAZPACHO

Chilled, fresh gazpacho is cooling and delicious served on a hot summer night. If it's paired with guacamole and chips, there's no need to turn on a flame and sweat to make dinner. Rachel Vaughn's recipe is a perfect blend of summer and spice. For the gazpacho, try to dice or mince the vegetables very tiny—about 1/8 inch if possible. They still stay crunchy and individual, but the flavors marry together better.

SERVES 6

- 3 cups Knudsen's Very Veggie spicy juice*
- 3 medium to large tomatoes, seeded and diced small
- 1 small jalapeño pepper, finely minced
- 1/2 cup finely diced red bell pepper
- 1/2 cup finely diced yellow bell pepper
- 1/2 cup finely diced orange bell pepper
- 2 tablespoons minced sweet onion, such as Vidalia, or red onion
- 2 medium cucumbers, peeled, halved lengthwise, seeded, and diced fine
- I large clove garlic, pressed through a garlic press
- 1 teaspoon chopped fresh basil, plus whole leaves for garnish
- 3 to 4 tablespoons finely chopped fresh chives
- 2 to 3 teaspoons sugar
- 1 teaspoon grated lemon zest
- 2 tablespoons freshly squeezed lemon juice, or more to taste
- 2 to 3 tablespoons extra-virgin olive oil
- Salt and freshly ground black pepper
- Hot sauce, to taste

In a large bowl, combine the spicy veggie juice, tomatoes, jalapeño, bell peppers, onion, cucumber, garlic, basil, chives, 2 teaspoons sugar, lemon zest, lemon juice, 2 tablespoons olive oil, and salt and pepper to taste. Taste the gazpacho and make any necessary adjustments in the amounts of lemon juice, sugar, olive oil, and salt. Add additional hot sauce if you would like it spicier. Chill for at least 3 hours or add some ice cubes if you need to serve it sooner. Garnish with basil leaves.

* Knudsen's organic Very Veggie juice is available in the whole or health food sections of grocery stores as well as in natural foods stores.

PAIR WITH SIDE ON PAGE 176.

SIDE GUACAMOLE AND CHIPS

You can always add spices such as cumin and chili powder or chopped cilantro to the guacamole if you like it zestier. It's best to prepare guacamole just before serving it.

SERVES 4

3 just-ripe avocadoes

1 clove garlic, finely minced

1 to 2 tablespoons freshly squeezed lime juice

1 small garden tomato, seeded and diced very small

2 tablespoons finely minced sweet onion, such as Vidalia

Salt, to taste

Tortilla chips

Cut the avocadoes in half, remove the pit, and spoon out the flesh. Place the flesh in a bowl and mash well with a fork. Add the garlic, 1 tablespoon lime juice, tomato, onion, and salt to taste. Taste with a chip, and check for seasonings. Adjust to taste. Serve on a platter with the chips.

PAIR WITH SOUP ON PAGE 175.

`SOUP` TOMATO SOUP

This is the simple, creamy tomato soup that kids and adults love to eat.

SERVES 6

2 tablespoons extra-virgin olive oil

1 onion, diced

1 whole leek, trimmed, cut in half
   lengthwise, rinsed, and sliced

1 teaspoon minced garlic

2 (28-ounce) cans whole tomatoes,
   with juices, seeded*

4 cups water

1 teaspoon chopped fresh thyme leaves

1 1/2 teaspoons sugar

1 to 2 teaspoons kosher salt

1/2 cup heavy cream

1 Heat the oil in a large soup pot over medium heat and sauté the onion and leek for 10 minutes, stirring occasionally. Add the garlic and stir until fragrant, 1 to 2 minutes.

2 Add the tomatoes, water, thyme, sugar, and salt and bring to a boil. Reduce the heat, cover, and simmer about 15 minutes, or until onion is thoroughly cooked.

3 Blend the soup in a blender until smooth. Return to the pot, stir in the cream, and taste for seasonings.

* I usually try to remove at least some of the seeds from canned whole tomatoes. Empty a can of tomatoes into a strainer (fine enough to catch the seeds but large enough to let the juices flow through) set over a bowl to catch the juices. Quickly open each whole tomato and let the seeds fall into the strainer. As you finish with each tomato, place it in the bowl and then push out the rest of the juice. Break up the tomatoes with your hand.

PAIR WITH SIDE ON PAGE 180.

SIDE HERBED CHEESE SANDWICHES

You can make these with regular sliced white bread or a favorite multigrain bread. To make the cheese sandwiches a bit different, try varying the cheese. Cheeses that work nicely include sharp cheddar, Gruyère, Fontina, Cantal, and Mahon.

SERVES 4 TO 6

1 tablespoon chopped fresh oregano
  or parsley

1 tablespoon chopped fresh basil

1 tablespoon extra-virgin olive oil, plus
  more for pan

1 small clove garlic, pushed through a
  garlic press

4 ounces cheese, such as cheddar,
  sliced about 1/4 inch thick

8 slices of bread

Butter, for the pan

1 In a small bowl, mix the oregano or parsley, basil, olive oil, and garlic together. Spread mixture on one side of 4 pieces of bread.

2 Place cheese slices in a single layer atop the herb mixture. Top with the second slice of bread.

3 Heat a large skillet over low heat and melt some butter and olive oil to coat. Cook the sandwiches until the bread is golden on both sides, flipping halfway through, and the cheese is melted. To ensure that the cheese melts, cover the pan while the sandwiches cook.

PAIR WITH SOUP ON PAGE 179.

SOUP RUSTIC FALL TOMATO SOUP WITH ORZO AND MINI MEATBALLS

This soup was created to use extra fall tomatoes and leeks that I had on hand. I had never quite realized how wonderful the combination of chicken stock and fresh tomatoes is; you could use this combo as a base for many variations.

SERVES 6

MEATBALLS:

3/4 pound 80-percent-lean ground beef*

1/3 cup fresh bread crumbs (any bread you have in the house, crumbled in a food processor)

1/4 cup water

1/3 cup grated Parmigiano-Reggiano cheese

1 clove garlic, finely minced

1/2 teaspoon dried oregano

2 tablespoons minced fresh parsley

3/4 teaspoon kosher salt

1/4 teaspoon freshly ground black pepper

SOUP:

2 whole leeks, trimmed, cut in half lengthwise, rinsed, and thinly sliced

2 tablespoons extra-virgin olive oil

2 cloves garlic, minced

5 fresh tomatoes (2 1/2 to 3 pounds), seeded and diced, or 1 (28-ounce) can diced tomatoes, with juices

6 cups chicken stock (preferably homemade)

3 cups lightly packed baby spinach

2 cups cooked orzo (about 3/4 cup dried)

1/2 teaspoon kosher salt, or to taste

Grated Parmigiano-Reggiano cheese, to taste

1 Preheat the oven to 375°. To make the meatballs, mix all ingredients together. Roll into balls up to 1 inch in diameter. Place meatballs on a baking sheet, and set aside.

2 To make the soup, sauté the leeks in the oil in a soup pot over medium-high heat for about 10 minutes. Lower heat to low, add garlic, and cook another 2 to 3 minutes. Add tomatoes and chicken stock and bring to a boil. Lower to a simmer, cover, and cook until the tomatoes are integrated into the soup, 10 to 15 minutes.

3 While the soup is simmering, bake the meatballs for 10 to 12 minutes, depending on the size (they don't brown up as much in the oven as they would sautéed in a pan, but that's okay).

4 Add the meatballs and spinach to the soup, and simmer another few minutes. Add the cooked orzo. Add the salt, and serve hot with a generous sprinkling of Parmesan cheese in each bowl.

* I have made these meatballs with ground turkey and they work great. With turkey, it's best to sauté the meatballs in a skillet rather than bake them in an oven.

PAIR WITH SIDE ON PAGE 182.

SIDE CROSTINI WITH GOAT CHEESE AND ROASTED PEARS

This makes a tasty fall side dish for soup or chili, or even a stand-alone appetizer for the holidays. The pears need to be roasted the same day they are being served, without being refrigerated.

SERVES 8

2 just ripe pears, such as Anjou

2 teaspoons extra-virgin olive oil

1/2 teaspoon chopped fresh thyme leaves

1 loaf fresh bread, such as cranberry-walnut or pecan bread

1 (4-ounce) package goat cheese, room temperature

1 Preheat the oven to 375°. Line a baking sheet with parchment paper. Peel the pears, cut them in half and scoop out the cores with a spoon or a melon baller. Rub each pear with olive oil. Place pears cut side down on prepared baking sheet, sprinkle with fresh thyme, and bake until lightly browned on the cut side and easily pierced with a fork, about 20 minutes. Remove from oven and let cool.

2 Slice each pear half into 3 or 4 slices. Turn the oven down to 350°.

3 Slice the bread 1/4- to 1/2-inch thick. Spread each slice with goat cheese. Lay 2 or 3 pear slices on top. Set aside on a baking sheet.

4 Just before serving, heat the crostini in the oven for about 10 minutes, to warm them up slightly.

PAIR WITH SOUP ON PAGE 181.

SUMMER

SOUP CHILLED CUCUMBER SOUP WITH GAZPACHO SALSA

The base of this light and very refreshing cold soup is a creamy combination of cucumber, avocado, and yogurt. The topping is a mini gazpacho-like salsa. This soup can be served as a first course at a nice summer meal or as an appetizer in demitasse cups. It goes nicely with mini fish or lamb skewers, smoked salmon on rye, or most simply, the crispy pita chips.

SERVES 5 OR 6

4 to 5 cucumbers (about 2 pounds)

1 cup water

1/2 cup plain yogurt, low-fat or Greek style

1 avocado, peeled and pitted

1/4 cup freshly squeezed lime juice

Salt and freshly ground black pepper

SALSA:

1 small cucumber

6 radishes, thinly sliced and cut into fine matchsticks (1/4 cup)

1 medium tomato, seeded and finely diced (about 1 cup)

1/4 red onion finely diced (about 1/4 cup)

1 tablespoon freshly squeezed lime juice

1 tablespoon extra-virgin olive oil

Salt

2 tablespoons finely chopped chives

10 to 12 basil leaves, slivered

1 Peel the cucumbers and cut in half lengthwise. With a spoon, scrape out and discard the seeds. Cut cucumbers into chunks and place in a blender. Add the water, yogurt, avocado, lime juice, and salt to taste. Blend until smooth. Taste and adjust the salt and amount of lime juice. Add a few grinds of pepper. Place in the refrigerator to chill, 2 hours.

2 To make the salsa, peel the cucumber, slice it in half lengthwise, spoon out the seeds, and cut into very small dice. Combine cucumber with the radish matchsticks, diced tomato, red onion, lime juice, olive oil, and salt to taste. Place in the refrigerator until ready to serve.

3 Just before serving, mix the chives and basil into the salsa. Ladle the soup into bowls. Top each helping with a generous spoonful of salsa.

PAIR WITH SIDE ON PAGE 188.

SIDE BAKED PITA CHIPS

These crispy pita chips are quite simple to make. You brush them with olive oil and top with a Middle Eastern spice condiment called za'atar, a combination of toasted sesame seeds and dried herbs like oregano, marjoram, thyme, and salt. Some versions include sumac, a lemony-flavored spice found in Middle Eastern stores. You will have some za'atar topping left over for additional batches.

MAKES ABOUT 30 PITA CHIPS

2 (5- or 6-inch) pita rounds
1 tablespoon dried oregano
1 tablespoon dried thyme
1 tablespoon sesame seeds, toasted
1/2 teaspoon sumac (optional)
1 teaspoon kosher salt
1 tablespoon extra-virgin olive oil

1 Preheat the oven to 350°. Line a baking sheet with parchment paper. Cut the pita rounds in half, then cut each half into 3 triangles. Separate the 2 pita layers and place on prepared baking sheet.

2 In a small bowl, combine the oregano, thyme, sesame seeds, sumac (if using), and salt.

3 Brush the rough side of each pita triangle with olive oil and sprinkle with a pinch or two of the za'atar. Bake until the pita chips are lightly crisp and golden, 6 to 8 minutes.

PAIR WITH SOUP ON PAGE 187.

SOUP ROASTED CHERRY SOUP WITH CRUSHED SUGARED ALMONDS AND MASCARPONE

This soup tastes as wonderful as it sounds. The flavor of the fruit is enhanced with a quick roasting and the presentation is elevated with the toasted almonds and the beautiful contrast of the mascarpone. It makes a light, easy dessert on a summer night. The recipe comes from Rachel Vaughan, a friend and talented private chef, who made the soup one night using some leftover roasted cherries, and loved the results.

SERVES 4 FOR DESSERT

4 cups dark red cherries (about 2 pounds), pitted*

5 tablespoons sugar, more or less depending on the sweetness of the cherries

2 teaspoons olive oil

Salt

3/4 cup cold water

2 teaspoons cornstarch

1/3 cup freshly squeezed orange juice

Grated zest of 1 lemon (about 1/2 teaspoon)

4 tablespoons mascarpone cheese, room temperature

2 tablespoons light cream

CRUSHED ALMONDS:

1/2 cup whole almonds, roughly chopped in the food processor

2 teaspoons butter, melted

1 tablespoon sugar

2 pinches of kosher salt, or to taste

1 Preheat the oven to 375°. Place pitted cherries on a baking sheet. Sprinkle with 1 tablespoon of the sugar, the oil, and 1 to 2 pinches salt. Mix well and roast for about 20 minutes. Set aside. Reduce the oven temperature to 250°.

2 In a small saucepan over medium-high heat, combine the cold water with the cornstarch and the remaining 4 tablespoons sugar. Bring to a simmer and let simmer a few minutes until slightly thickened.

3 Place the roasted cherries with all their juices in a blender. Add the orange juice, lemon zest, and about 2/3 of the cornstarch mixture. Blend until almost creamy, leaving a little texture. Taste, and adjust the thickness with additional water or orange juice if needed. The mixture should be a bit thinner than pancake batter. Chill until ready to serve.

4 To prepare the almonds, place them on a sheet pan with the butter and sugar and mix well. Sprinkle with a few pinches of salt. Bake until nicely roasted and crunchy, 10 to 12 minutes. Keep a close eye on them so they don't burn.

5 In a small bowl, whisk together the mascarpone with light cream. Add additional cream if needed to create a thick but pourable consistency.

6 To serve, spoon the soup into small bowls. Add a nice swirl of the mascarpone mixture. Sprinkle with a generous topping of the crushed almonds.

* Pit cherries by hand by gently pulling the cherry almost apart and scooping out the pit with your index finger.

PAIR WITH SIDE ON PAGE 192.

SIDE SUMMER FRUIT SKEWERS

The fruit on these skewers can be varied according to what's in season. Look for short appetizer skewers. If you can't find them, you can cut regular bamboo skewers with scissors.

SERVES 4

4 to 8 skewers
1/2 pint raspberries
1/2 pint blueberries
1 pint strawberries, cut in half
4 to 8 cherries
8 small mint leaves

Skewer the fruit by carefully adding a raspberry, 2 blueberries, a strawberry, a cherry, and 2 mint leaves. Serve each person 1 or 2 skewers.

PAIR WITH SOUP ON PAGE 190.

SOUP CHILLED WATERMELON SOUP

Just a whirl in the blender with fresh watermelon and a hint of lime, and the soup is finished. The garnish is a Greek-based salsa of sorts with cucumber, olives, feta, and fresh herbs. Try it on its own as a first course or brunch starter, or grill a skewer of shrimp to accompany.

SERVES 4 TO 6

7 cups seedless red watermelon chunks

4 tablespoons freshly squeezed lime juice

1/2 small to medium cucumber, peeled, seeded, and diced very small

1/2 cup kalamata or green olives, pitted and chopped

1/4 red onion, diced very small

1 tablespoon extra-virgin olive oil

Pinch of kosher salt

2 tablespoons chopped fresh mint

2 tablespoons slivered fresh basil

3/4 cup crumbled feta cheese, such as Valbresso sheep's milk feta

1 Cut 1 cup of the watermelon chunks into small dice; set aside. Place the remaining 6 cups watermelon and 3 tablespoons of the lime juice in a blender and blend until smooth.

2 In a bowl, combine the diced watermelon, cucumber, olives, red onion, the remaining 1 tablespoon lime juice, and the olive oil. Season with a pinch of salt.

3 Just before serving, ladle the watermelon soup into bowls. Gently place a generous spoonful of the watermelon salsa on top. Add a sprinkling of herbs and a bit of cheese to each bowl.

PAIR WITH SIDE ON PAGE 195.

SIDE SKEWERED HERB SHRIMP

Straightforward, simple, and delicious.

SERVES 4

3 tablespoons extra-virgin olive oil

2 tablespoons minced fresh parsley

1 tablespoon minced fresh chives

1/2 pound small to medium shrimp, peeled (leaving the tails on), and deveined

Salt and freshly ground black pepper

4 skewers

1 Heat an indoor grill, grill top, or outdoor grill. In a small bowl, mix together the olive oil, parsley, and chives. Add the shrimp and season with salt and pepper.

2 Skewer the shrimp, 3 to a skewer. Grill about 2 minutes per side. Serve immediately.

PAIR WITH SOUP ON PAGE 193.

SOUP MINTED HONEYDEW MELON SOUP WITH COCONUT SORBET

With a pretty lime-green color and specks of mint, this chilled soup makes an easy, light dessert on a hot summer night, especially when paired with lime spice cookies. Garnish with 2 mini scoops of your favorite sorbet; coconut, mango, raspberry, and blackberry are all delicious.

SERVES 6 FOR DESSERT

1 honeydew melon (about 4 pounds), cut into pieces (about 5 cups)

3 tablespoons freshly squeezed lime juice

1 tablespoon freshly squeezed lemon juice

1 packed tablespoon fresh peppermint leaves

Coconut or raspberry sorbet

Mint leaves, for garnish

1 Place the melon, lime juice, lemon juice, and mint together in a blender and puree until smooth and speckled with the green mint. Chill until ready to serve.

2 Ladle or pour melon soup into small dessert bowls. Using a melon scooper, scoop out 2 or 3 balls of the sorbet of your choice and lightly place on top. Garnish with a mint leaf or sprig.

PAIR WITH SIDE ON PAGE 198.

SIDE LIME SPICE COOKIES

These rich, buttery, shortbread-like cookies offer a hint of lime and delicate spice. The recipe comes from Lisa Zwirn, a friend, Boston-based food writer, and the author of *Christmas Cookies: 50 Recipes to Treasure for the Holiday Season*. After making the lemon-lime melon soup, I asked Lisa if she would create a special cookie recipe to accompany it. Here is the delicious result.

MAKES ABOUT 55 COOKIES

1 cup (2 sticks) unsalted butter, room temperature

3/4 cup sugar

1 large egg yolk

2 packed teaspoons finely grated lime zest (from about 2 limes)

1/2 teaspoon pure vanilla extract

2 cups all-purpose flour, plus more for dusting

1/4 teaspoon kosher salt

1/2 teaspoon ground ginger

1/2 teaspoon freshly grated nutmeg

1 Using an electric mixer, beat the butter in a large bowl until creamy. Add the sugar and beat until fully blended. Beat in the egg yolk, then the lime zest and vanilla.

2 In a separate bowl, whisk together the flour, salt, ginger, and nutmeg. With the beaters on low speed, add the dry ingredients to the butter mixture, beating just until fully combined. The dough should be crumbly but will feel moist when pinched. Gather the dough into a ball, then divide it in half.

3 On a lightly floured surface, form one half of the dough into a rough log shape, then roll it back and forth to form a smooth cylinder about 10 inches long and 1 1/4 to 1 1/2 inches in diameter. Roll up the log in plastic wrap and secure with an outer layer of foil. Repeat with the remaining dough. Refrigerate the logs for a few hours or freeze until firm. (The logs can be frozen for up to 2 months.)

4 Preheat the oven to 350°F. Line a cookie sheet with parchment paper. Working with one log at a time, cut the dough into 1/4- to 1/3-inch thick slices. Place the rounds on the prepared sheet, arranging them about 1 1/2 inches apart. Bake until the cookies are a pale golden color, a little browner around the edges, about 13 minutes. Carefully transfer the cookies to a rack to cool.

PAIR WITH SOUP ON PAGE 196.

SOUP CHILLED STRAWBERRY SOUP WITH PROSECCO

Prosecco is a reasonably priced Italian sparkling wine, and a favorite drink of mine. I love to add it to various fruit soups for a little pizzazz. This elegant starter course really tastes best when local strawberries are in season. I sometimes serve it as part of a group of appetizers by pouring it into narrow appetizer glasses or demitasse coffee cups.

SERVES 6 TO 8

4 cups strawberries, hulls removed

1/2 to 1 cup Prosecco or sparkling water

1/4 cup sugar, or more to taste

1/3 to 1/2 cup freshly squeezed orange juice

2 teaspoons freshly squeezed lime or lemon juice

Lemon or lime sorbet

In a blender or food processor, pulse the strawberries, 1/2 cup of the Prosecco, the sugar, the orange juice, and the lime juice; the mixture should be slightly chunky. Adjust the consistency with additional Prosecco if needed. Refrigerate until ready to serve. When the soup is chilled, taste it and adjust the sugar or lime juice depending on the sweetness of the strawberries. Garnish with a tiny scoop of sorbet.

SIDE LEMON-HERB RICOTTA DIP

This dip is easy to make and tastes especially delicious if you have fresh ricotta cheese on hand.

SERVES 6 TO 8 AS AN APPETIZER

1 1/2 cups ricotta cheese

1/4 teaspoon kosher salt, or to taste

1/2 teaspoon freshly ground black pepper

1 teaspoon lemon zest

1 teaspoon chopped fresh thyme

1 tablespoon extra-virgin olive oil

Crackers, crostini, or grilled bread for dipping

In a medium bowl, combine the ricotta cheese with the salt and half of the black pepper, lemon zest, and thyme. Transfer the dip to your serving bowl, and garnish with the remainder of the black pepper, zest, and thyme. Drizzle with the olive oil and serve with crackers or grilled bread.